Future Trends from Past Cycles

Identifying share price trends and turning points through cycle, channel and probability analysis

by Brian J. Millard

HARRIMAN HOUSE LTD

3A Penns Road
Petersfield
Hampshire
GU32 2EW
GREAT BRITAIN

Tel: +44 (0)1730 233870
Fax: +44 (0)1730 233880
Email: enquiries@harriman-house.com
Website: www.harriman-house.com

First published in Great Britain 2010 by Harriman House

Copyright © Brian Millard

The right of Brian Millard to be identified as the author has been asserted
in accordance with the Copyright, Design and Patents Act 1988.

ISBN: 978-1-871857-04-7

British Library Cataloguing in Publication Data
A CIP catalogue record for this book can be obtained from the British Library.

Printed and bound in the UK by CPI, Antony Rowe.

"The further back you can look, the farther forward you can see."

Winston S. Churchill

About the Author

Brian J. Millard's background was as a scientist and until 1980 he was a senior lecturer at the University of London, publishing over 70 scientific papers.

He later became interested in the work of J. M. Hurst on cycles and channels in the stock market and, as this interest grew, spent time carrying out research in this field. Following his landmark book *Stocks and Shares Simplified*, published in 1980, Brian wrote a further five books on the application of scientific methods to the stock market.

His books on channel analysis are now universally recognised as taking forward the work of J. M. Hurst to a higher level by analysing price movement and especially the occurrence of predictable cycles in market data. Brian also published software to enable traders to apply his methods.

Other Books by Brian Millard

Quantitative Mass Spectrometry
Stocks and Shares Simplified: A Guide for the Smaller Investor
Traded Options Simplified
Millard on Channel Analysis: The Key to Share Price Prediction
Profitable Charting Techniques
Winning on the Stock Market
Channels & Cycles: A Tribute to J. M. Hurst

Brian Millard (1937-2009)

Brian worked tirelessly for the last two years, building on his earlier research and publications, to create the theories and techniques contained within this book. He died very suddenly in July 2009 before he could see the publication of this work.

I don't have a record of the many who helped in validating and testing the work presented – but I thank you for your contribution.

I would especially like to thank Martin Smart, who gave up his time to proof this work for my father, and Louise Hinchen at Harriman House, who has given me such support in bringing this book to you.

A great intellect and passion has been taken from the world; it is a lesser place for the loss.

Sandy has lost a wonderful husband, Alastair and I the best dad anyone could have, and his grandchildren – Rebecca, Eleanor, Madeline and Edward – a grandpa who was so proud of them.

I hope that this book brings you much success with your investments.

Simon Millard

Northampton, October 2009

Contents

List of Figures

List of Tables

1

Introduction

It is now just about ten years since I wrote my last book, *Channels & Cycles: A Tribute to J.M. Hurst*. I have been gratified by the response I have had to that book and the many kind comments I have received about my approach to trading on the stock market.

I still acknowledge that Hurst set me on the road along which I have been travelling since that time in 1979 (is it really 30 years ago?) when I picked up his book *The Profit Magic of Stock Transaction Timing*. This book was reprinted by Traders Press in 2000, and I urge readers to take advantage of its restored availability. For those around when it was first published in 1971 it was a breath of common sense in showing what is possible when approaching the markets with a measured, logical technique based on firm mathematical and scientific logic. New readers will see it in a different light, because now there are many authors and many software packages that use these important principles. To these new readers it might not now appear as revolutionary as it did when first published, but they will still enjoy Hurst's writing style and the book's logical approach to the improved timing of buying and selling decisions.

When considering a title for this book, I started by thinking about what goes through a trader's mind when contemplating a trade. It is usually: 'I think the price of this security will rise/fall within n hours/days/weeks/months.' The thought process of a much smaller number of traders will be: 'There is a high probability that the price of this security will rise/fall within n hours/days/weeks/months.'

Provided the second type of trader has carried out his analysis carefully, he will in the long run be more successful than the first type of trader.

You can now see my dilemma in choosing the title for this book. Should I stress the novelty aspect of using cycles in a way that hasn't been attempted before, or should

I stress the importance of making sure that probability is always on your side? In the end I opted for novelty, being aware that novelty is always appealing.

Readers of my books on channel analysis will be aware that the most difficult aspect of that technique is in deciding when a channel has changed direction. How the channel has behaved in the gap between its last calculated value (half of the span used to calculate it back in time from the present) is open to interpretation. It is this which has been the subject of my research over the last ten years and which lies behind my writings in this book.

In *Channels & Cycles* I made the point that channel analysis could be carried out with a paper and pencil and that a computer was not strictly essential. However, the study of cycles and their relationship to channels has now moved on so much that a computer is absolutely essential. Some of the scans of cycles that I will describe take tens of millions of calculations to perform and quite clearly a fast computer is therefore essential.

Except for the cycle scans described in this book that are unique to the packages Channalyze and CCS Visions, the isolation of single cycles can be performed by any software package that allows you to specify your own calculations. These types of calculation can also be carried out in a spreadsheet application such as Microsoft Excel. Of course, in all of these cases a good amount of accurate historical data is required so that long-term cycles can be studied.

Channels can be drawn by Channalyze, but for other software packages a paper and pencil can still be useful for drawing constant depth channels based on a centred moving average which has been calculated by the computer software. These constant depth channels should not be confused with Bollinger bands, which virtually all software packages can produce. Bollinger bands are not of constant depth and, unlike channels, bear no obvious relationship to cycles.

I chose the title *Future Trends from Past Cycles* because it clearly describes what the book is all about. Although no mention is made of channels in this title, channels are an essential part of taking an investment decision. The channel is based on the future trend, but knowledge of the future trend does not in itself give the trader the optimum time to place a trade. I took a rather different approach in *Channels & Cycles*, placing more weight on a discussion of channels and less on cycles. The balance in this book is reversed, since quite clearly all channels are derived from cycles, or rather sums of cycles.

Definition of a Trend

Different readers will have different perceptions of what constitutes a *trend*. There are many uses of this word in technical analysis. There is, however, one property that is often overlooked, but which is essential, and that is a timescale. Each trend should have a timescale associated with it. Once this is accepted, then it is perfectly reasonable to separate trends into short-term, medium-term and long-term.

Definition of a Cycle

A perfect cycle in the market is a sine wave. Associated with the sine wave is a wavelength, measured in minutes, hours, days, weeks, years, etc and an amplitude. The amplitude is measured in whatever units the security is quoted, such as points for an index, a ratio for foreign exchange and currency units such as pounds, dollars and euros for stocks. A third parameter is the phase, which is how far along the cycle is from some arbitrary starting point. We will see later that sine waves are described by an equation, which allows us to know its future path provided we know the three parameters which are unique to that particular sine wave.

Unfortunately, market cycles are not stable throughout their lifetime, and their amplitude will change after a period of time, rendering predictions unreliable. The way around this dilemma is to use only those cycles which have been stable for a short period of time and should remain so in the near future.

Determining Trends

The title of this book explains what it is all about. It is to determine as far as possible the future direction of a trend of interest, whatever its timescale. The title also explains that this can be done by an analysis of cycles present in market data. While stable-cycle analysis is the prime method, it is only one of the three analyses which must be carried out before a decision is taken about the future direction. These three analyses are:

1. Cycle analysis: determining those cycles which are currently stable and adding the appropriate cycles in order to estimate the future path of the trend. The current stability of the cycle sum is checked by means of a comparator, a centred nine-day moving average.

2. Channel analysis: confirming that the trend estimated by the cycle sum is supported by channel analysis.

3. Probability analysis: confirming that the trend is also supported by an analysis of the predicted probable price range a few days into the future.

Following this sequence of analyses, the ideal situation will be when a predicted change in direction of a trend is imminent and is likely to happen a few days into the future. The progress of the estimated trend can then be followed each day as more price information arrives. If the new information indicates that the trend estimation is beginning to vary from the initial prediction, then move to another security.

Before taking a position in the security, it is essential that the change in direction is confirmed. Because of the fact that market cycles are constantly varying, changes in direction must never be anticipated.

Trend position

Naturally, an estimation of a future trend will be liable to an uncertainty in its position over the course of time. This is illustrated in Figure 1.1.

Figure 1.1 – There will be an uncertainty in the location of the central trend line.

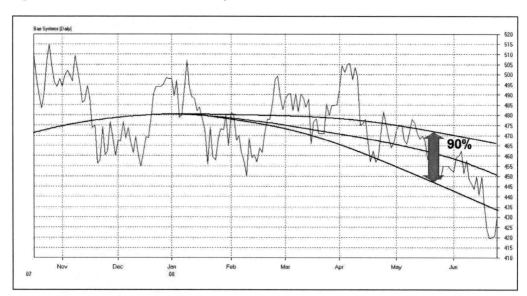

In the example shown in Figure 1.1 there is a 90% probability that the trend line lies between the two positions indicated by the vertical arrow.

Price position

Once we have determined the likely position of the trend, our attention will turn to the relationship between the value of the security, stock, index or foreign exchange ratio, and the estimated position of the trend. In my previous work on

> **" Before taking a position in the security, it is essential that the change in direction is confirmed. "**

channel analysis I showed that the values of securities oscillate around a central trend and that there is a limit to this oscillation. This limit depends upon the timescale of the trend and differs from one security to another.

We will be able to draw probability boundaries that will give the probability of a price being at a particular place *relative* to a predicted central trend. This concept is illustrated in Figure 1.2.

Figure 1.2 – Probability boundaries if we assume that the central trend is in the correct position. In this case there is a 95% probability that the price lies between the two boundaries.

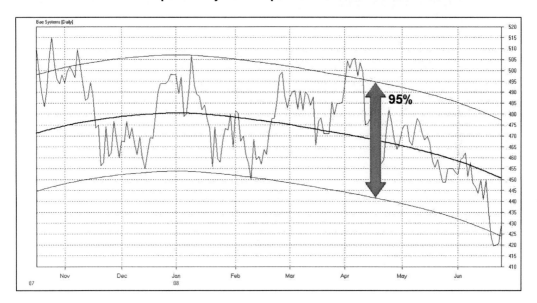

In the example shown in Figure 1.2 the boundaries are placed at a point where there is a 95% probability that the price lies between these two. In fact we will see later that the probability of the price being at an exact position relative to the boundary changes as we move between these two boundaries can be determined at least approximately.

When we are at, say, the lower boundary there is a high probability (but *not* 100%) that the price will rebound upwards. This means that there is a low probability that the price will fall further. Conversely, when we are at the upper boundary there is a high probability (but *not* 100%) that the price will fall back. This means that there is a low probability that the price will rise further. These boundaries are at a constant vertical distance apart throughout the whole set of data. Thus they form a constant depth channel, which is the basis of *channel analysis*. The probabilities are calculated from the distances between the value of a centred moving average at each point and the price at that point. A more exact explanation of the change in probability across the channel will be given in a later chapter.

Combining these two probabilities

It can now be seen that the prediction of the future movement of a price depends upon knowing the probable position of the future trend and the position of the price value within the constant depth channel constructed around this trend. If we use p(price) to be the probability of a future value for the stock price, p(trend) to be the probability associated with the trend position and p(relative) to be the probability of the price position relative to the channel boundaries, then it follows that:

```
p(price) = p(relative) x p(trend)
```

Based on a great deal of research into channel analysis, a reasonably accurate value can be obtained for the probability relative to the central trend (p(relative)). This is provided of course that an extensive amount of historical daily closing data is available for the particular stock, currency or commodity. The greater the amount of data, the more accurate is the value obtained. At least 1000 points must be considered to be the minimum required.

We will see later that at the present state of development of cycle prediction, we can arrive at only an approximate probability for (p(trend)), i.e. the future position of the central trend.

This is because, unlike the p(relative) calculation, which is based on real data and real values for the moving average which have been used, the future cycles are themselves estimates. They are based on the assumption that a stable cycle will remain stable for a reasonable time into the future. However, as we have mentioned, cycles will change both in amplitude and wavelength. This change will add uncertainty to the estimated future position of each cycle and therefore to the estimated sum of cycles.

More about probability

Probability is rarely discussed in books on technical analysis, most likely because it appears to be an academic topic which is difficult for the lay person to understand. However, this depends upon how the topic is addressed, and whether it is absolutely essential to the understanding of the rest of the book. I have taken the view that it can be addressed in a simplified way that will make it easy for the lay person to grasp the important fundamentals and that it is not necessary to concentrate on terrifying equations with integral signs and exponential terms to achieve this.

It should be stressed here that it is not essential that the reader should grasp clearly the subjects of statistics and probability in order to profit

❝ You will not be 100% correct in your decision making. ❞

from this book. These topics are addressed purely so that the reader can understand that there is a mathematical underpinning of the issues that are discussed later. There are many texts available and many snippets on the internet that have the objective of making statistics and probability more easily comprehensible to the layperson. Thus readers may, if they wish, skip over those chapters which discuss probability. Of course, the calculations require data, and sources of data in the correct format for using in spreadsheets and at no cost to the user are widely available online. For readers who would prefer to access these probability calculations by a quicker route, they are also available in the Channalyze program.

If the trader does not remain disciplined and forgets about making sure that probability is on his or her side, then failure is the almost certain outcome. Just like the casinos in Las Vegas, in the long term you will win if the odds are on your side. It only takes a small shift in the odds in your favour to improve your performance out of all recognition. Conversely, a small shift the wrong way can lead you to despair. It is essential to monitor the trend prediction constantly to make sure that a cycle that will cause an adverse shift in these trends is not rapidly gaining in amplitude.

One final message – you will not be 100% correct in your decision making. There is no such thing as a cast iron, guaranteed profit in stock, commodity or currency markets.

2

Risk and the Markets

In my previous book (*Channels & Cycles*) I spent some time in the first chapter discussing money management. This is an important subject for traders and many have come unstuck owing to a failure to divide their capital into a number of parts which are traded in different stocks. I have always suggested dividing into eight, but certainly into not fewer than six. This means a total loss in one trade, while painful, can be accommodated. The discipline to stay with this partition of capital must be maintained at all times. Never put more than this one part into any one position, however positive the outcome might look at the time the trade or investment is being considered. Quite obviously the existence of risk means that there is never a trade which has 100% probability of success. Even those with a 90% probability of profit still have a 10% probability of failure and there will be many occasions in your life as a trader where the outcome that is only 10% probable is the one which occurs. You are bound to make a loss in some trades, so make sure you are not wiped out by it through lack of discipline.

The minimum strategy might be said to preserve capital at all times. This seems to be a negative approach since the aim of a trader or investor should be to increase capital over a period of time. A much more positive approach can be achieved by the quite simple strategy of applying probability to maximise profit and reduce losses.

Sources of Risk

The risk to the performance of a stock comes from several sources, and the trader must be aware of these so that a rounded view can be taken at all times. The net performance of the stock is the result of all these influences. As far as the individual stock is concerned, there are a number of influences that can affect the stock price.

Individual stock

There is the risk to the price of an individual stock due to a deteriorating performance of the company that it represents. This performance may involve a cut in the dividend, to which investors do not take too kindly. It might take the form of an announcement about future prospects with the usual comment about difficult trading conditions over the coming year. It might involve an obvious drop-off in sales, a failed takeover bid for another company or for the company itself, paying too high a price for another company, or the purchase of another company which is likely to under-perform in the immediate future. There will be other risks, but the above will serve to give a good overall view.

Market risk

The old Chinese saying 'a falling tide will maroon all boats' is very apposite when applied to the other risks: those of the sector, the whole market, worldwide markets and major political events.

The trader must keep more than a weather eye on these other influences. If the sector of which the stock is a member is becoming unfashionable, then it is unlikely, although not impossible, that any individual stock will outperform the sector. However, the balance of probability is that the odds are against any large increase in the stock price unless there are special circumstances such as a takeover that can be identified. Thus it will be useful to maintain, and indeed analyse, a chart of the sector index, just as one would analyse the individual stock.

It goes without saying that the major market index should be constantly monitored. If the market is headed strongly downwards, then it is unlikely that an individual stock will continue to move in the opposite direction for any appreciable length of time. This is easily checked by looking at the advances and declines in stocks in the financial pages the next morning after an above average fall in the market.

" There is never a trade which has 100% probability of success. "

The other side of this coin is when a stock in which you are invested does not rise with the rest of the market. This is particularly galling, but can be mostly avoided if the principles shown in this book are followed.

Link between individual daily stock prices

It is interesting to examine the behaviour of individual stocks from different market sectors to see if changes in one stock are reflected by changes in another stock. In the London market the three stocks AstraZeneca, Jardine Lloyd Thompson and Tesco were examined. These are from very diverse sectors – pharmaceuticals, holiday travel and food retail. Thus in the absence of a stock market, it can be assumed that these stocks would be rising or falling quite independently of each other. If they are not totally independent of each other, then this must be due to the influence of the market itself upon overall investor sentiment, which manifests itself in a degree of synchronisation between stocks.

The closing prices of these three stocks were studied for the period from the beginning of 2003 to February 2009, a total of 1597 individual daily values. The daily changes of each of these were then calculated, giving 1596 such values for each stock. The assumption was then made that the daily changes within each stock were independent of each other. The relationship between the daily change in one stock with each of the other two was examined. In other words, if the price of AstraZeneca fell on a particular day, did the prices of Jardine Lloyd Thompson and Tesco also fall? If the price of one rose on a particular day, did the prices of the others also rise? Logic would dictate that this is most unlikely, so the test boils down to: what proportion of the 1596 changes were in the same direction for two or all three of these stocks? The results are shown in Table 2.1.

Table 2.1 – Daily changes in AstraZeneca, Jardine Lloyd Thompson and Tesco from 2003 to 2009.

Stock	Rises	Falls
AstraZeneca	784	812
Jardine Lloyd Thompson	738	858
Tesco	728	868

Table 2.2 – Synchronised daily changes for AstraZeneca (AZN), Jardine Lloyd Thompson (JLT) and Tesco (TSCO).

Stock	Total changes	Synchronised	Percentage
AZN/JLT	1596	943	59
AZN/TSCO	1596	1002	63
JLT/TSCO	1596	921	58
AZN/JLT/TSCO	1596	635	40

If the behaviour of these three stocks is totally independent, then we would expect the prices to move in the same direction 50% of the time. If only a small number of changes were taken, then the result could differ from the value of 50% due to the effect of probability. However, with a large number such as 1596 the actual percentage of synchronised movements should be close to 50%. The values of 40, 58, 59 and 63 are sufficiently removed from 50% that it can be considered that these movements are not totally independent, but show a small measure of dependence upon each other. Where does this dependence come from? It comes of course from the overall effect of the market.

While the effect of the market over the long term (a period of about six years was used for the study shown in Table 2.2) is not very large, over the shorter term it will be much more important. Large changes in the market will cause the majority of stocks to move in the same direction. The figures in Table 2.2 reflect the fact that over the long run, there are only a few such large changes in the market, the rest being of such low magnitude that they have only a minimal effect.

The effect of various changes in the market, as measured by an index, on the behaviour of individual stocks is illustrated in Figure 2.1. Here the change in the market index over various three-month periods is plotted against the change in the individual stocks over the same period.

Figure 2.1 – The relationship between the performance of individual stocks and the market itself over three-month periods. The vertical axis is the percentage of rising stocks. This shows that once the percentage rise or fall in the index exceeds 10%, the majority of stocks follow suit.

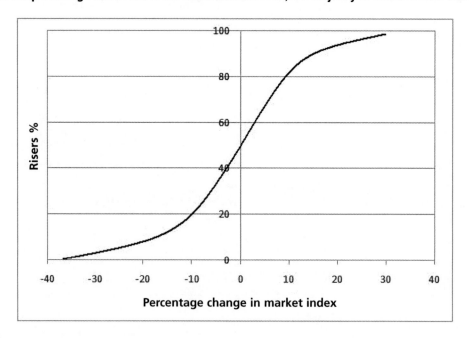

The relationship shown in Figure 2.1 is interesting – it is of course not a straight line. When the index has more or less stood still over a three-month period, then around half of the stocks rise and half of them fall over this same period. For changes of 10% or more in the index in a three-month period, then the majority of stocks follow suit in rising or falling. It is this relationship which makes it difficult to buck the market during periods of high volatility, such as that which we experienced during the 2007–2009 crisis.

World markets risk

Investors in the major markets around the world should always take note of what the other major markets are doing. Thus although London might be doing very well up until 2:30pm UK time, a major fall on Wall Street at the opening will see London respond in a negative fashion. This can be very frustrating for UK investors who might find that the price of a stock that has no connection whatsoever with the United States suddenly goes into reverse simply because of the behaviour of Wall Street. The opposite is of course also true in that a large fall in London up until lunchtime will frequently cause a fall at the opening of Wall Street.

The behaviour of major world markets over the period from the end of October 2008 to the end of January 2009 is shown in Table 2.3.

Table 2.3 – Change in some world markets over three months from the end of October 2008 to the end of January 2009.

Country	Index	30/10/08	30/01/09	% change
Australia	All Ords	4017.9	3540.7	-11.9
China	Hang Seng	13968	13278	-4.9
France	CAC 40	3487.0	2973.9	-14.7
Germany	DAX	4987.9	4338.3	-13.0
Japan	Nikkei	8576.9	7994.0	-6.8
UK	FTSE 100	4377.3	4140.6	-5.4
US	DJIA	9336.9	8000.8	-14.3

Whilst there is a wide variation in the percentage fall in the markets shown in Table 2.3, the fact is that they all fell over this period. Taking the general relationship from Table 2.3, it can be seen that the approximate percentage of rising stocks in each of these markets would be as shown in Table 2.4. The best of these markets was China, where only 68% of stocks fell during the period. The worst was the United States, where 90% of stocks fell during the period. In terms of probability, there is no doubt that the odds were stacked against the trader during this time. Naturally, within this period there will have been short-term rises in most of these stocks, with some rises being insignificant, while others would have been quite useful. A short-term trader could therefore have made profitable trades over a period when the overall change was unprofitable.

Table 2.4 – Approximate percentage of rising stocks over the period from the end of October 2008 to the end of January 2009.

Country	Index	Percentage rises
Australia	All Ords	18
China	Hang Seng	32
France	CAC 40	10
Germany	DAX	17
Japan	Nikkei	25
UK	FTSE 100	28
US	DJIA	10

The message from this is to tailor your trading horizon to match the timescale of the trend that has been identified. However, there is no doubt that if the medium-term trend is downward, then the profit from short-term trades will be far, far less than if the medium-term trend is upwards. This issue of the timescales of various trends is of course addressed in a later chapter.

Political events such as an interference with oil supplies can have a major effect on all markets. If such events happen, the trader who can quickly see the implication is the one who will benefit the most, provided he or she takes the appropriate action.

It is difficult to put a numerical value of probability on those risks which have just been highlighted as being outside of those due simply to the stock itself. However, in monitoring the stock price over a period of time we will be able to determine at least approximate probabilities of the range of future movement.

London and Wall Street daily closes

The same exercise as was performed on AstraZeneca, Jardine Lloyd Thompson and Tesco can be performed on the closing values of London (FTSE 100) and Wall Street (DJIA). This is shown in Table 2.5.

Table 2.5 – Daily changes in closing values for FTSE 100 and DJIA. The 'Next day' column is for synchronisation of the FTSE 100 Index with the previous day's close of the DJIA.

Index	Total days	Rises	Synchronised	Next day
FTSE 100	2296	1134	1127	1176
DJIA	2296	1120	1127	

In this exercise the value in points of the rise or fall has been ignored and only whether both markets have risen or both markets have fallen is noted. Thus out of 2296 daily changes, 1127 were synchronised. If pure chance was operating, then the expected number of synchronisations would be half of the total, i.e. 1148. The actual value of 1127 is close enough, given the large number of changes being taken into account, to arrive at the conclusion that there is virtually no synchronisation between daily rises and falls if the level of the rise or fall is ignored. Since Wall Street closes well after London, the final column notes the behaviour of London the following day, when the previous day's performance of Wall Street is known to London traders. The level of synchronisation is still that which would be expected from purely random behaviour.

However, just as large changes in a market will affect the majority of stocks in that market (as we saw in Figure 2.1), then we can understand how sometimes one market can influence another if enough traders are taking note of other markets. This can be evaluated by studying the effect of unusual rises or falls in Wall Street on the behaviour of the London market the next day. The situation is clouded rather by the overlap of the trading sessions. Thus if Wall Street falls one day by a large amount, then London will usually follow suit the next morning. However, if Wall Street then rises at the start of the next session, then London may recover some of the ground lost in the morning session.

Show in Table 2.6 are the rises and falls in London which follow the direction of Wall Street the previous day, versus the percentage rise or fall in Wall Street. This enables us to determine at what level a change in Wall Street is very likely to affect the London market the next day.

Until we get to a level of around 2.5% of movement in the DJIA, then the effect on the next day's movement in London is minimal. However, once we see movements of 3% and above we see an increasing effect on London stocks, with around three-quarters of stocks moving in the same direction.

The question then arises as to whether Wall Street is affected by a large change in London on the same day? This is shown in Table 2.7.

Table 2.6 – Daily changes in the DJIA greater than the specified percentage and whether London moved in the same direction the next day. The data was obtained over 2300 days.

DJIA change greater than (%)	Number of days it occurred	FTSE days same direction	FTSE days same direction (%)
1.0	703	393	56
1.5	384	220	57
2.0	216	137	63
2.5	126	87	69
3.0	78	53	68
3.5	54	40	74
4.0	38	29	76
4.5	28	21	75
5.0	17	13	76

Table 2.7 – Daily changes in the FTSE 100 Index greater than the specified percentage and if Wall Street moved in the same direction the same day. The data was obtained over 2300 days.

FTSE change greater than %	Number of days it occurred	DJIA days same direction	DJIA days same direction (%)
1.0	711	369	52
1.5	400	213	53
2.0	222	124	56
2.5	141	75	53
3.0	80	43	54
3.5	57	32	56
4.0	39	25	64
4.5	31	20	64
5.0	20	10	50

Tables 2.6 and 2.7 are interesting in that the number of days (out of 2300) that these various percentage changes occurred were very similar, e.g. for greater than 2% there were 216 days in the Dow and 222 days in the FTSE 100 Index. It also has to be acknowledged that traders in the US take less notice of what happens in London than traders in London do about New York. It is not until London movement gets to 4% and above that New York stocks start to see an effect, causing a larger percentage of them to move in the same direction.

In conclusion, being aware of the behaviour of other markets in the short term will help the trader to avoid placing buying and selling orders on a day when these external forces will increase the probability of an adverse move in the particular stock of interest.

3

How Prices Move (I)

In this chapter we will need to understand the concept of probability at a very simple level. This simple introduction will be very helpful in understanding the issues in Chapter 4.

Probability can be expressed either as a percentage or as a fraction. The difference is simply that a fractional probability is multiplied by 100 in order to arrive at the equivalent percentage probability.

In mathematics, a probability of an event X is represented by a number in the range from 0 to 1 and written as p(X). A probability of 0 means that the event is impossible, while a probability of 1 means that the event is certain. Thus if X is the event where a zero is thrown on a dice, then p(X) = 0; the event is impossible because there is no zero on a six-sided dice.

If we take a six-sided dice as an example, there is only one face out of six with a particular number such as a three. Thus the probability of throwing a three, p(3), is 1/6, which is 0.166 or 16.6%.

If we wish to link two events together, such as rolling two dice, the probability of a certain outcome is simply the probabilities of each single outcome multiplied together.

Thus, as we have stated, the probability of throwing a three on a dice is 1/6. The probability of throwing a three on the second dice is also 1/6. Thus the probability of throwing two threes is 1/6 x 1/6 = 1/36 or 0.0277 (2.77%). Quite low!

Mathematically, if we call the second event Y, then its probability is p(Y). Thus the probability of both events X and Y happening is given by:

```
p(X) x p(Y)
```

In general, therefore, if we wish to see the outcome of a certain number of events, then the probability of all of these happening is obtained by multiplying together all of the individual probabilities. Those readers who wish to exercise their minds further could check out the probability of drawing a flush in five-card poker (all five cards of the same suit). This is very low!

One important point – the probability of an event not happening (call it p(not X)) is (1 minus the probability of it happening). Thus, using our p(X) for the probability of the event happening, the probability of it not happening is given by:

$$p(not\ X) = 1 - p(X)$$

From this, we can see that the probability of not throwing two sixes will be 100 - 2.77 = 97.23%

Various probabilities of everyday occurrences are shown in Figure 3.1.

Figure 3.1 – The probabilities associated with the occurrence of various outcomes.

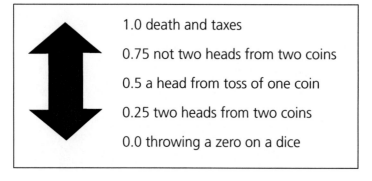

1.0 death and taxes

0.75 not two heads from two coins

0.5 a head from toss of one coin

0.25 two heads from two coins

0.0 throwing a zero on a dice

Coin Tossing

Most people are confused by the probability of an event such as the next toss of a coin resulting in a head if there has already been a sequence of heads. In the toss of a coin each toss is independent of the previous toss, so that even if a sequence of ten successive heads has been achieved, the chance of the next throw being a head is still 50%. The coin, being inanimate, has no knowledge of its previous history.

Sequence of tosses

The probability of the next toss achieving a head or a tail is not the same as determining the probability of a sequence of, say, heads or tails before the coin tossing experiment begins. The probabilities of runs of successive heads can be determined by multiplying together the probabilities of each event.

Thus, probability of tossing:

- 1 head = 0.5 (50%)

- 2 heads = 0.5 x 0.5 = 0.25 (25%)

- 3 heads = 0.5 x 0.5 x 0.5 = 0.125 (12.5%)

- 4 heads = 0.5 x 0.5 x 0.5 x 0.5 = 0.0625 (6.25%)

And so on.

Note that the probability of achieving, say, five heads is exactly the same as the probability of achieving four heads and then a tail. If the required outcome is three successive heads, then the expected proportion is 12.5%. As the number of tosses increases, then the proportion that is actually achieved settles towards the expected value. Since 1000 tosses is a reasonably large number, then the sequence of three heads should occur fairly close to 125 times in 1000 tosses. In other words the most likely value is 125 times, but since by their very nature tests based on probabilities do not give exact, repeatable outcomes then a value close to 125, rather than exactly 125, might be obtained.

It is possible to arrive at a probable range for the outcomes of such experiments using standard deviation. This is a measure of the scatter of a set of measurements around a mean value. The two words 'accuracy' and 'precision' can be used in this context. Accuracy refers to how close the mean of a set of results is to the true value, while precision refers to the scatter about the mean value. It is better to be roughly accurate than precisely wrong. A set of measurements with high precision will have a small standard deviation. However, it cannot be deduced from this that the mean of the results is closer to the true value than the mean of another experiment in which the standard deviation is higher.

In coin-tossing experiments, the larger the number of tosses, the closer will the end result be to the true result. This can be seen from the formula for standard deviation in coin-tossing experiments:

```
standard deviation = 0.5 * square root (N)
```

where N is the number of tosses. Thus for the number of heads in 1000 tosses, the standard deviation is 15.8. From the properties of a normal distribution (see later) this means that 95% of the occurrences of heads will lie within a range of 16 (15.8 rounded up) either side of the expected value of 500. Note that the standard deviation from sets of numerical data is obtained by a more complex formula, but that it is not necessary to apply such a formula since the standard deviation is easily obtained by using a spreadsheet program (this function is usually named STDEV) or many technical analysis programs.

As far as stock markets, currency markets or commodity markets are concerned, in this book we are only concerned with the probability of one event occurring over a specified period of time and that is whether our security is going to rise or fall. We shall see in a later chapter how to obtain probabilities from moving averages. Even though we use these in quite a simple way, they will be the rock on which our trading strategy of predicting trends in these markets is built.

Rising and Falling Trends

A rising trend can be considered to be a sequence of changes after which the end value is higher than the starting value, a falling trend one in which the end value is lower than the starting value, and a sideways trend one in which the end value is the same as the starting value. There has to be a timescale attached to these trends, the time being the number of changes in the sequence. In this book we are not concerned with intra-day data, so all our data is based on daily values.

There are two aspects of trends that can be considered. A rising trend will occur if we have a sequence of successive rises, irrespective of the amount of each rise. In other words, only the direction is important. A rising trend will even occur if there is not a sequence of successive rises, but if the sum of the individual rises is greater than the sum of the individual falls. The opposite applies to falling trends. We can study these two aspects using simple applications of probability.

Sequence of rises and falls

If we take the data for AstraZeneca – which was used earlier to study the correlation between movements in AstraZeneca, Jardine Lloyd Thompson and Tesco – we will see that there were 784 rises, 749 falls and 63 no changes out of 1596 daily changes.

The question arises as to whether we can predict with any certainty whether the next day's close will be higher, lower or unchanged from the day before. Of course, we addressed in Chapter 2 the issue of large changes in Wall Street having an effect on London stocks the next day, so that in these special circumstances we saw that we could be correct around 75% of the time. Later in this book we will see how to predict whether a short-term trend is expected to change direction. However, it will become clear that we cannot pin this change of direction down to the exact day. We will only be able to confirm the change once it has happened and we certainly should not open a trade until we have this confirmation.

It is helpful in this discussion to examine more closely these rises and falls in AstraZeneca. Note that there is nothing special about AstraZeneca (apologies to any readers who are holders of that stock!) – the same conclusions will be reached from a study of any other stock, currency or commodity from any other market.

In simple terms, we can say that since there were 784 rises out of 1596 daily changes, the probability of a rise after the period covered by this set of data would be 784/1596 = 49%. To be more correct, we should say that the likelihood of a rise is 49%. Just as in the simple coin-tossing experiment we would only get approximately 50% heads out of a trial of 1000 coin tosses. This is because the issue of standard deviation comes into the picture. Thus the actual probability lies somewhere within a range of values around this value of 49%. However, for our purposes, taking just the likelihood of a rise is sufficient for us to be able to take the discussion forward.

The value of 49% means that there is a more or less equal chance that the price will rise or the price will fall.

We can calculate probabilities from the data as follows:

- Probability of a rise = 784/1596 = 0.494

- Probability of a 'not rise' = 1 - 0.494 = 0.506

- Probability of a fall = 749/1596 = 0.469

- Probability of a 'not fall' = 1 - 0.469 = 0.531

- Probability of no change = 63/1596 = 0.039

- Probability of change = 1 - 0.039 = 0.961

From these probabilities we can, just as in the case of the coin-tossing experiment, calculate the probabilities of seeing isolated successive rises, isolated successive falls or isolated successive 'no changes' in the history of daily changes. By isolated we mean that a rising sequence is ended by a fall or 'no change' movement, a falling sequence by a rise or 'no change' movement and a 'no change' sequence by a rise or fall. It is important to study isolated sequences; otherwise the issue would be confused, since a sequence of four successive rises would also contain two sequences of three successive rises.

Thus, the probability of four successive rises, started by a 'not rise' and ended by a 'not rise':

= 0.506 x 0.494 x 0.494 x 0.494 x 0.494 x 0.506 = 0.0152

Since we have 1596 daily changes, this should lead to 0.0152 x 1596, which gives 24 such sequences.

The probability of four successive falls:

= 0.469 x 0.469 x 0.469 x 0.469 x 0.531 = 0.0257

Since we have 1596 daily changes, this should lead to 0.0257 x 1596, which gives 41 such sequences.

The probability of four successive 'no changes':

= 0.039 x 0.039 x 0.039 x 0.039 x 0.961= 0.000002

This gives a probability of effectively 0 for such sequences.

A careful analysis of successive rises, falls and no changes in AstraZeneca gives the results shown in Table 3.1. The sequence of one covers the case where there is an isolated rise, fall or no change. In a sense this would not be a sequence, but is still of interest and so has been included.

Table 3.1 should be compared with the expected values, calculated as shown above for a sequence of four rises, falls and no changes. These are shown in Table 3.2.

Table 3.1 – Sequences of isolated rises, falls and no change in AstraZeneca over a period of 1596 daily changes.

Sequence	1	2	3	4	5	6	7	8
Rises	192	84	52	30	16	6	4	2
Falls	200	96	44	26	11	5	4	1
No change	40	10	1	0	0	0	0	0

Table 3.2 – Expected sequences of isolated rises, falls and no change in AstraZeneca over a period of 1596 daily changes.

Sequence	1	2	3	4	5	6	7	8
Rises	201	100	49	24	11	6	3	2
Falls	210	99	46	21	10	5	2	1
No change	57	2	0	0	0	0	0	0

The actual sequences of two or more are so close to the expected values that it must be considered that the next day's move is independent of the previous day's move.

The implication is therefore that sequences of rising or falling daily changes are almost totally random. If these sequences are the only driving force for uptrends or downtrends then it would follow that trends are random and therefore traders may as well pick their positions with a pin. However, the other dimension to a trend is the extent of each upward or downward move, which will be investigated later in this book.

One last aspect of sequences of rises and falls to investigate is whether there is any relationship between the sequence of rises or falls and the total change in value over the length of time for which the sequence holds.

The relationship between the total rise and length of rising sequences is shown in Figure 3.2. Also drawn on the plot are the straight-line trends of these data. It can be seen that the rises are a good fit to this straight-line trend and therefore the price rise is essentially directly proportional to the length of the sequence. In other words, if we break down rising sequences into an average change per day, then long sequences do not give a different rise per day from that of short sequences.

Figure 3.2 – The relationship between total price rise and sequence length.

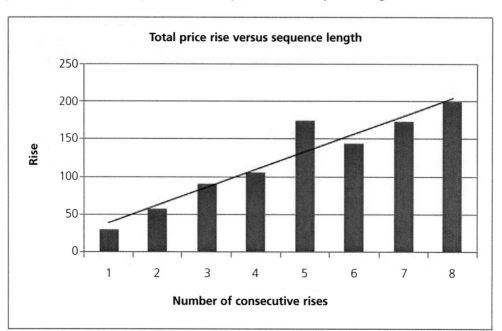

The relationship between the total fall and length of falling sequences is shown in Figure 3.3. Also drawn on the plot are the straight-line trends of these data. It can be seen that the falls are a good fit to this straight-line trend and therefore the price fall is essentially directly proportional to the length of the sequence.

In other words, if we break down falling sequences into an average change per day, then long sequences do not give a different fall per day from that of short sequences.

Figure 3.3 – The relationship between total price fall and sequence length.

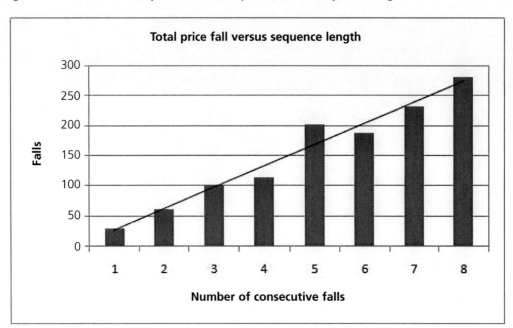

The results of the studies in this chapter would lead to the conclusion that price changes are random, since the number of successive rises or falls in a sequence are simply those that would be expected if there is an equal probability of a rise or fall each day. However, the next chapter will show that when it comes to putting values on daily changes rather than simply examining the direction of the change, we will see that they do not conform to a random distribution and therefore the prediction of future price levels is still possible.

4

How Prices Move (II)

The application of probability to sequences of rises or falls, even though of interest, was a rather trivial use of probability. When we come to the numerical values of these changes, we need to examine how probabilities can be arrived at by studying the distribution of price changes. By distribution we mean an analysis of the way in which the data is scattered about the mean value. It is necessary to introduce the statistical concept of the normal distribution in order to understand what can be deduced from a study of the actual value of the daily changes.

Note that it is not necessary to carry out laborious calculations – this can be done quite simply in a spreadsheet.

The Normal Distribution

As an example, the average height of men in the United States is 69.1 inches (175.5cm) with a standard deviation of 2.9 inches (7.4cm). Quite obviously, there are men shorter and men taller than this, but a survey of the population would find that the vast majority of men would have heights close to this value. As we move away from this average value, the numbers of men with that particular height gets fewer and fewer.

The plot of numbers of men in a particular height category would appear as shown in Figure 4.1. The data falls into what is called a normal distribution around the mean of 69.1 inches. The standard deviation is a measure of the scatter of the data around the mean value. A fundamental property of the normal distribution is that:

1. 68% of the data falls within +-1 standard deviation of the mean

2. 95% of the data falls within +-2 standard deviations of the mean

3. 99.7% of the data falls within +-3 standard deviations of the mean.

Using the value of the standard deviation given in inches, this means that 68% of the men in the United States have heights in the range 66.2 to 72.0 inches and 95% of them have heights in the range 63.3 to 74.9 inches.

Since standard deviation is easily calculated in a spreadsheet such as Excel (using the STDDEV function), then the value of the normal distribution is that we can now state quite simply the limits between which 68% or 95% or 99.7% of the data will lie.

Figure 4.1 – This shows a plot of heights of men in the United States. The average height is 69.1 inches and the standard deviation 2.9 inches.

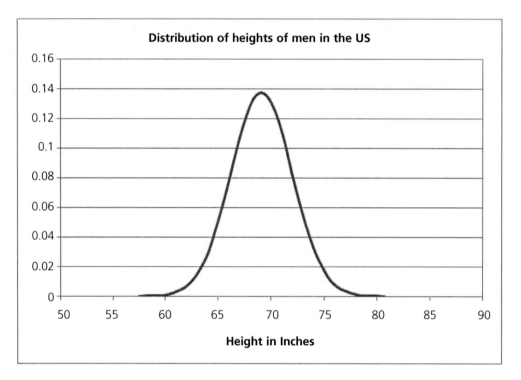

As we will see shortly, these limits are derived from areas under the distribution curve. They represent probabilities. Thus in this example the probability is that, in the United States, the next man you see in the airport or train or bus station will have a height of between 66.2 and 72 inches is 68%. The next time you are stuck in one of these public places, amuse yourself by taking your own mental and approximate survey.

Of course we have to be sure that the data we are examining are normally distributed. The simplest way is to plot the distribution and then see if it resembles a normal distribution such as that shown in Figure 4.1.

The standard normal distribution

What is called the standard normal distribution is a set of data with a mean of 0 and a standard deviation of 1. A plot of this data is shown in Figure 4.2.

Figure 4.2 – The standard normal distribution curve has a mean value of 0 and a standard deviation of 1. In this plot the x-axis represents standard deviations from -5 to +5. The shaded area represents the 95% probability limits for a future value.

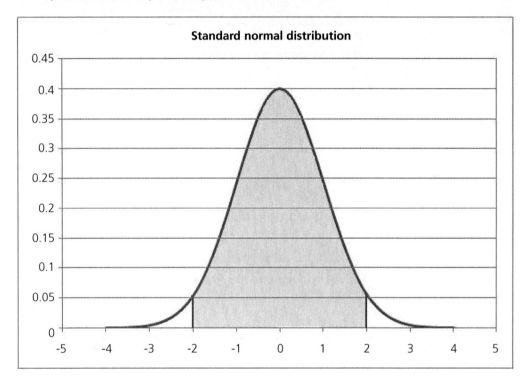

This is mentioned here because a value, x, from a normal distribution specified by a mean of μ and a standard deviation of σ can be converted to a corresponding value, z, in a standard normal distribution with the transformation $z = (x - \mu)/\sigma$. And, of course, in reverse, any value from a standard normal graph, say z, can be converted to a corresponding value on a normal distribution with a mean of μ and a standard deviation of σ by the formula $x = \mu + z^{*}\sigma$.

Thus readers who wish to compare actual distributions to normal distributions can bring both the same scales. We will see the value of this when discussing the spread of data around a centred average in Chapter 7.

However, there is a highly valuable property of the normal distribution that allows us to predict the range in which a price should move on any particular day. We mentioned earlier that:

1. 68% of the data falls within +-1 standard deviation of the mean

2. 95% of the data falls within +-2 standard deviations of the mean

3. 99.7% of the data falls within +-3 standard deviations of the mean.

This can be converted to a probability that any particular day's change will be within those limits if it is assumed that the prices are normally distributed. The shaded area in Figure 4.2 represents the 95% probability that a future price will lie between these limits. All we need to calculate this is the mean value and the standard deviation computed from a reasonable amount of historical daily changes.

Converting distributions to probabilities

The probabilities we have used so far have involved simply the probability levels of 68%, 95% and 99%. How do we find the probability of data lying between two values, or being greater or less than a specified value? The answer lies in the fact, which we have already mentioned, that it is the area under the distribution curve that gives us the probabilities. The probability of a data point lying between two values is obtained by taking the area under this curve as a proportion of the total area under the curve. Thus in Figure 4.2, the shaded portion under the curve lies between the values of +- 2 standard deviations. The area of this is exactly 95% of the total area under the curve. We therefore need a way of converting the normal distribution curves to a more usable probability curve. This is done by plotting the cumulative area as we move from the left to the right of the plotted data.

Calculating the area under the normal distribution curve is not a trivial process and involves a mathematical integration. However, a good enough approximation can be obtained by using the bin technique in a spreadsheet program or in Channalyze. This involves dividing the range along the x-axis into a number of equal segments (bins). The corresponding y value for each bin is then calculated for the normal distribution. All of these separate values can be summed to give a good approximation of the total area and the sum between two bin values will give the partial area of interest.

This process is illustrated in Figure 4.3. In this case 32 bins have been used to cover the range from -4 to +4 standard deviations. Quite obviously, the greater the number of bins into which we divide the x values, the closer will the end result approach the true profile of the normal distribution.

Figure 4.3 – The area under the distribution curve can be approximated by adding up the values in each of the bins. The bins are of width 0.25 of a standard deviation.

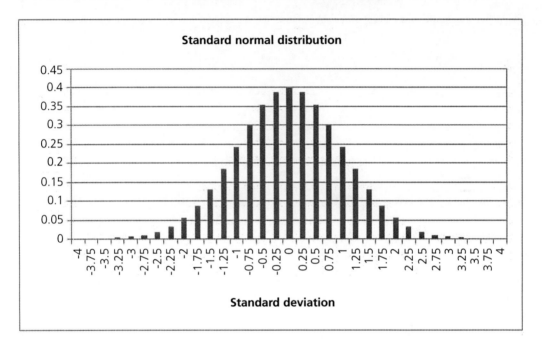

If we build a running total of the values in the bins as we move from left to right of this plot, and plot this total against the bin number, then we get a good approximation of the cumulative distribution. This will give us the plot shown in Figure 4.4.

Figure 4.4 – The cumulative distribution derived from the normal distribution shown in Figure 4.3. The y-axis now depicts the probability, on a scale of 0 to 1, that a point from the distribution is greater than a value on the x-axis. At the value of 0 for standard deviation the probability is 0.5 (50%), i.e. there is an equal chance of the point being greater or less than this value.

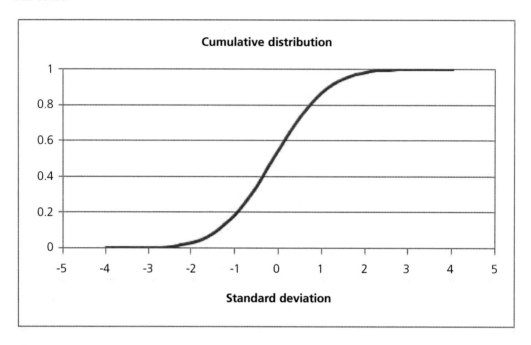

For any value along the x-axis, the corresponding y-value will give the probability that a new point from the distribution will be less than the value on the y-axis. By the time we reach the mid-point at 0 standard deviation, this probability is 0.5 (i.e. 50%), i.e. there is an equal chance of the new point being higher or lower than the mean value, which in this case is of course 0.

The normal distribution of stock price changes

We have already looked at the sequences of daily rises and falls in the AstraZeneca stock price. As far as the value of these changes is concerned, they range from a fall of 227p to a rise of 304p. The average value is -0.12, which for all intents and purposes can be taken to be 0. The standard deviation, which is a measure of the scatter of these changes around the average value, is 41.36.

Using the same method as for the normal distribution shown in Figure 4.3, i.e. just using the mean value and standard deviation and making the assumption that the data is normally distributed, we get the plot shown in Figure 4.5.

Since this is a plot of the normal distribution of AstraZeneca, its shape will be exactly the same as the distribution shown in Figure 4.3. The values on the x-axis will be different, since the mean is not 0 (it is -0.12) and the standard deviation is not 1 (it is 41.36).

Figure 4.5 – The normal distribution of AstraZeneca daily price changes based solely on the mean value of -0.12 and standard deviation of 41.36.

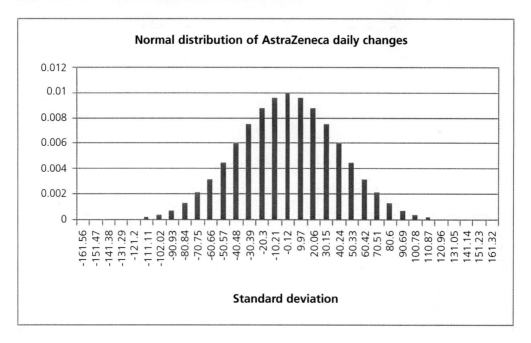

The cumulative distribution is the absolute key to determining the probability of a future point being less than or more than a certain value or indeed the probability of the future point being inside or outside of a range of values provided the data are normally distributed. The Channalyze program has a module which plots both the normal distribution and the cumulative distribution at the same time and allows the probability of any price change to be determined. This is shown in Figure 4.6. Here the values have been distributed into 60 bins and the cursor has been placed over the value for bin 26.

Figure 4.6 – The normal and cumulative distributions from AstraZeneca daily changes. Moving the cursor over the cumulative plot gives the probability that the price change will be less than the indicated value.

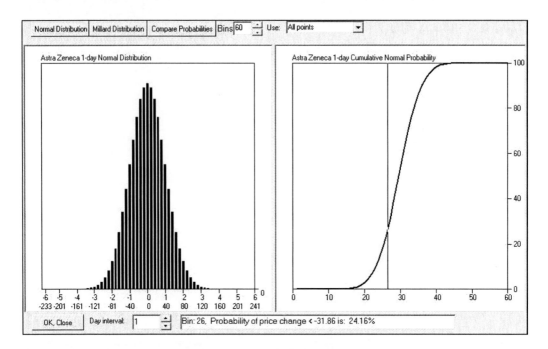

Bin 26 corresponds to a price change value of -31.86 and the corresponding probability is 24.16%. Since the values in the bin have been summed from the left-hand side, this means that the probabilities are for a future price change to be less than the indicated value. The probability that a future price change will be higher is obtained by subtracting this probability from 100, giving a 75.84% probability that the price change will be greater than -31.86.

The actual distribution of stock price changes

Daily changes

If we plot the distribution of the AstraZeneca daily changes by putting them into bins of width 10, running from -230p to 310p, we get the plot shown in Figure 4.7.

Figure 4.7 – The actual distribution of daily changes in AstraZeneca. The changes are allocated to bins of 10p running from -230p (fall) to +310p (rise).

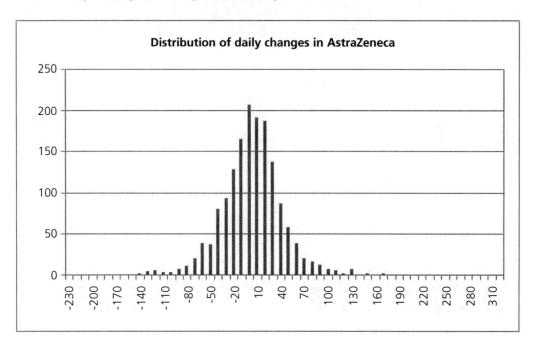

The question arises as to whether the distribution shown in Figure 4.7 is a normal distribution. The actual distribution is much higher in the middle relative to the tails than it should be for a normal distribution. Obviously it is not symmetrical and so we can say it is not exactly a normal distribution, but is it close to being a normal distribution? If we bring both of these plots from Figures 4.6 and 4.7 to the same scale and then take the difference between them we get the plot shown in Figure 4.8. This shows quite clearly the increased values from the middle of the distribution.

Figure 4.8 – The differences between the actual distribution of AstraZeneca daily price changes and what would be expected if these were normally distributed.

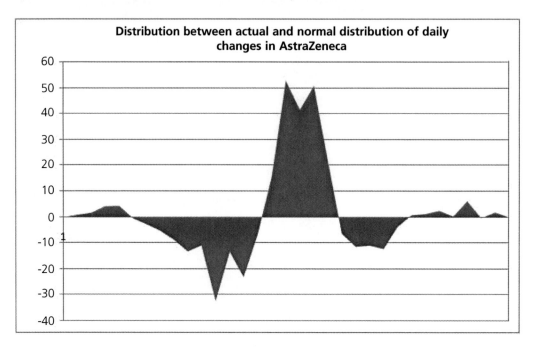

What this means is that the price changes in AstraZeneca are not randomly distributed. AstraZeneca was used as an example because it is a security quoted both in London and in New York. Other securities also behave in exactly this way. If prices are randomly distributed then the whole concept of technical analysis would be meaningless, since trend prediction would not be possible.

Now that we have decided that the actual price changes are not normally distributed, the question arises of whether or not we can still determine probabilities from this distribution. The answer fortunately is yes, since we can adopt the same approach that we used for the normal distribution of adding the values in each bin to give a cumulative plot. This gives the distribution shown in Figure 4.9.

Figure 4.9 – The actual distribution and cumulative distribution from AstraZeneca daily changes. Moving the cursor over the cumulative plot gives the probability that the price change will be less than the indicated value. In this case there is a 16.44% probability that the price change will be less than -29.66. This means there is a 70.34% (100-29.66) probability that the price change will be greater than -29.66.

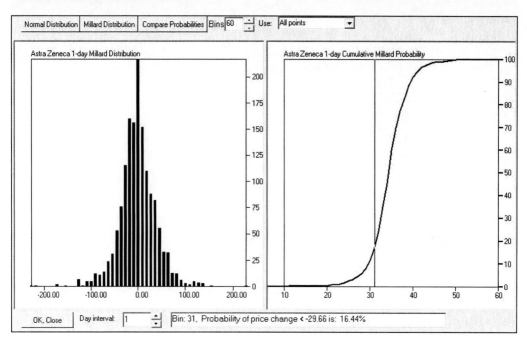

The curve is not as smooth as that shown for a normal distribution of the price changes, but that is of course because the plot of the actual distribution (Figure 4.8) does not have a smooth profile. The cumulative distribution simply reflects this fact.

Changes of more than one day

We can follow the principles used for calculating the distribution of daily changes to examine the distribution of changes which occur over periods longer than this. The data are obtained by the difference between each data point and the point n days further forward. As with daily changes, from this set of data a mean value and a standard deviation can be obtained. From this the normal distribution can be constructed via a spreadsheet. The normal distribution will have exactly the same shape as the normal distributions shown earlier in this chapter, as can be seen from Figure 4.10.

Figure 4.10 – The normal distribution of five-day changes in AstraZeneca (left panel). The right panel shows the cumulative distribution from which probabilities can be obtained.

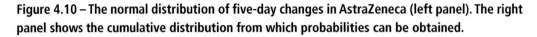

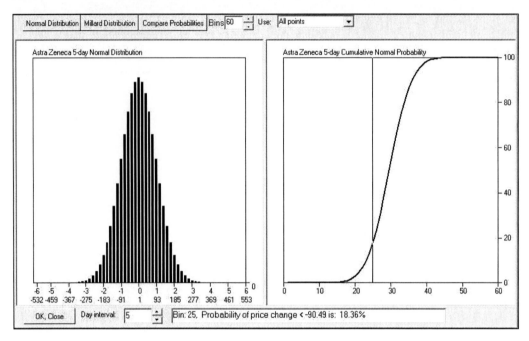

The cursor in this example has been placed at a point which shows the probability of a change of less than -90.49p over a future five-day period is 18.36%.

The actual distribution of five-day changes is shown in Figure 4.11. The interesting point here is that the actual distribution is much closer to the normal distribution shown in Figure 4.10 than is the case with one-day changes. However, the probability levels associated with the actual distribution are rather different. Thus the closest probability level that can be displayed to that of 18.36% in the normal distribution case is one of 19.83%. This is because only 60 bins have been used, giving a coarse control over the probability values. This level of 19.83% is the probability that the price change is less than -64.4p, considerably different from the value of -90.49 obtained for the normal distribution.

Figure 4.11 – The actual distribution of five-day changes in AstraZeneca (left panel). The right panel shows the cumulative distribution from which probabilities can be obtained.

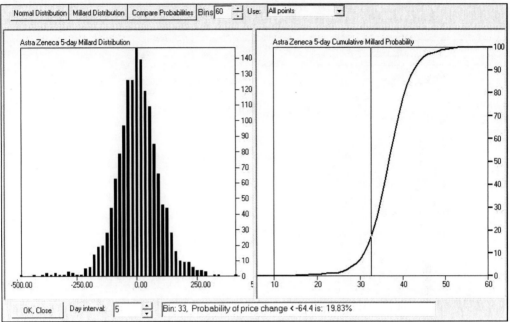

This method of estimating probable future movements is only valid for short periods of change, with five-day changes being a sensible upper limit. This can be demonstrated by taking an extreme value of change period and examining the distribution of the actual price changes. This is shown in Figure 4.12 for 151-day changes. It can be seen quite clearly that the structure has now disappeared, with a very large scatter about the mean. This of course means a large standard deviation, meaning that any prediction of a future price 151 days ahead will have such a large range as to be meaningless.

Figure 4.12 – The actual distribution of 151-day changes in AstraZeneca (left panel). The right panel shows the cumulative distribution from which probabilities can be obtained. It can be seen that now the distribution contains a wide range of changes of approximately similar probability.

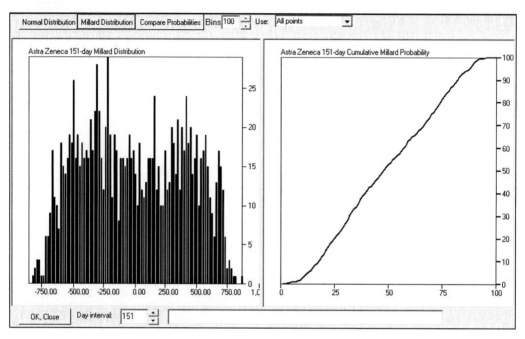

Why large periods cannot be used

The reason that the distribution of changes over periods of time greater than about five days loses its structure is because such changes use the same process as that used for moving averages. It will be seen in Chapter 10 that the value of a moving average depends on the value of the data point which is dropped and the value of the new data point which is brought into the addition. Thus the 151-day changes shown in Figure 4.12 are equivalent to examining the daily changes in a 150-day average. Since we know such averages to be much smoother versions of the original data, we can see why the distributions rapidly begin to differ from those when periods of up to around five days are used.

The overall message from this chapter therefore is that price changes of stocks over short periods of time are not random, since the distribution of price changes does not follow a normal distribution. Because of this, prediction of future prices over short time periods will give useful results with a limited probable price range. Once the period of time starts to exceed around five days, then the range becomes increasingly large so that predictions using this method are of limited value. However, this method is still extremely useful in determining the probability of a short-term trend changing direction, as is discussed in Chapter 10.

However, probabilities can still be derived over longer periods of change by using simulation, such as the Monte Carlo method. This is discussed in the next chapter.

5

Simulating Future Movement

We saw in the last chapter that using probabilities derived from the price change distribution was only valid for changes over a limited number of days. It is possible to construct probable movements over, say, a five-day period by taking probabilities from the individual daily changes as predicted from a normal distribution. Of course, we have already decided that daily changes are not normally distributed, but it is helpful to go through this exercise in order to clarify our thoughts about what is possible and what is not possible.

We pointed out earlier that one property of the normal distribution is that there is 95% probability that the next data point will lie within +- 2 standard deviations of the mean.

Thus, using this method on the AstraZeneca data, where the mean value is -0.12 and the standard deviation is 41.36, we arrive at the following range within which there is a 95% probability that the next price value will fall (the last price was 2393 on 23 February 2009):

1. lowest value = 2393 – (2 x 41.36) = 2310

2. highest value = 2393 + (2 x 41.36) = 2475

This therefore gives a range of four times the standard deviation for the next price, which is 7% of the last price. In other words there could be a rise of 3.5% or a fall of 3.5%.

Of course, if there is a 95% probability that the next day's change will lie between these two values, then there is a 5% probability that it will lie outside of these limits.

Since there are two such extremes, then there is a 2.5% probability that the price will be below 2310 and a 2.5% probability that the price will be above 2475.

If we look two days ahead then the position would be:

1. lowest value = 2310 - (2 x 41.36) = 2227

2. highest value = 2474 + (2 x 41.36) = 2556

In general therefore, the 95% limits for a future price are:

1. lowest value = latest value - (2 x number of days x standard deviation)

2. highest value = latest value + (2 x number of days x standard deviation)

If the limits for AstraZeneca are plotted for a number of days into the future, then these are seen to be straight lines, as shown in Figure 5.1.

Figure 5.1 – The future price for AstraZeneca will have a 95% probability of staying between these two straight lines if a normal distribution is assumed.

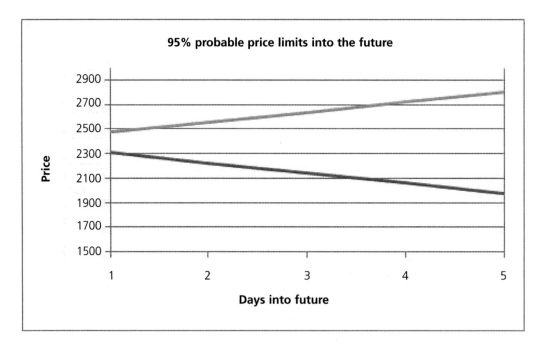

Although, as we have stated, the AstraZeneca price changes are not normally distributed, this way of looking at probabilities does give an approximate indication of the future movement. It should be pointed out that, although the range of price movement is approximated by this method, there is no indication of the direction of movement and it is this that is the subject of the remaining chapters in this book.

There is another way of tackling the issue of probability levels for future price movements over longer periods of time and that is by the simulation method.

Monte Carlo Simulation

Monte Carlo simulation is the process of using a set of random numbers and a number or numbers randomly selected from this set to generate an outcome. This outcome will be just one of an infinite number.

A good example of the use of simulation is to determine the value of π. By performing a large number of simulations (trials) the overall outcome will tend towards the true result.

Remembering Pythagoras' Theorem from our school days, this states that in a right-angled triangle the square of the hypotenuse is equal to the sums of the squares of the other two sides.

Figure 5.2 – The radius of the circle OA can be calculated from the vertical distance AB from the origin (y-value) and the horizontal distance OB from the origin (x-value).

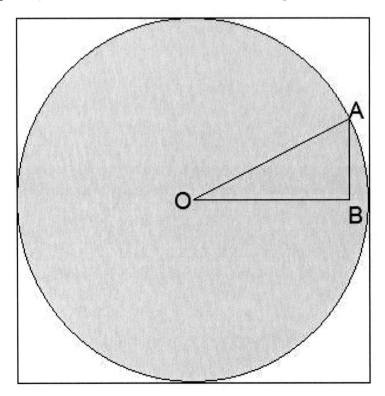

In Figure 5.2 we show a square with dimensions 2 units on each side, with a circle just touching the sides of the square. Thus the radius (r) of the circle is 1 unit. The area of this circle is πr^2.

Also shown is a triangle with its longest side (the hypotenuse) equal to the radius of the circle. However, this is the triangle with the longest possible hypotenuse to keep it inside the circle. We can of course draw other triangles in which the hypotenuse is outside the circle but inside the square.

As shown, from Pythagoras we get:

$$OA^2 = OB^2 + AB^2$$

If we use random values for OB and AB which lie between 0 and 1, then some of these will result in a value of OA which is equal to or less than the radius of the circle, while others will give a value of OA, which is larger than the value of the radius.

Now the area of the square is 4 units (2 units each side) and the area of the circle (with radius (r) = 1 unit) is πr^2, i.e. π. Thus the ratio of the area of the circle to the area of the square is $\pi/4$.

Now the problem can be boiled down to:

1. Take two random numbers, each between -1 and +1. Call these randX and randY.

2. Calculate $randR^2$ = the sums of the squares of each of these, i.e. $randR^2 = randX^2 + randY^2$.

3. Calculate $rand^2$ = square root of $randR^2$.

4. Compare randR with the required radius R (which is = 1).

5. If randR is greater than 1 then the random point lies outside of the circle. Otherwise it is in the circle.

6. Calculate π, which is = 4 x number of points inside/total points.

The more such trials are carried out, the closer will the result come to the value of π, which is 3.142 (to 3 decimal places). It should be noted that this is not the method of choice for calculating π, since it has been calculated to many thousands of decimal places by powerful computer programs. However, as an introduction to the Monte Carlo method it is extremely informative. Note also that to get accurate values is very demanding of computer time, since the error in the result improves by the square root of the number of trials. Thus to reduce the error by a factor of 100 would require 10,000 times the original number of trials.

Millard version of Monte Carlo simulation

The usual Monte Carlo method as applied to option pricing uses the normal distribution from which to select a random value to use in a calculation. In the Millard version of the method the numbers from which a selection is made are not a set of random numbers but the set of price changes which have actually occurred historically. In the last chapter we saw that these changes, for example in the case of AstraZeneca, were not normally distributed but had a bias towards the smaller price changes.

The method can be thought of as putting into a pot all the possible price changes which have occurred historically and then removing one at a time randomly from the pot. The first value taken is added to the last real price value to give the price after day one, the next value taken from the pot is used to give the price after day two and so on. This moves the estimated price into the future, for example, 30 days. This first exercise (one simulation) is then but one of the very large number of possibilities for price movement. In order to arrive at a more meaningful result, a large number of simulations (trials) are repeated, each of course with a different outcome for future movement. These outcomes (trials) will form a distribution, just as was the case in the last chapter where distributions of actual price movements for AstraZeneca were shown. While the actual price distribution is limited by the amount of historical data available, the Millard Monte Carlo distribution is only limited by the number of trials that are carried out. From these trials an estimate is made of the probabilities of the future price being within certain ranges, for example the 95% probability range as was calculated for AstraZeneca using the normal distribution method.

Figure 5.3 shows the result of simulating the five-day changes in AstraZeneca using 2000 trials. The 95% probable price change is from -298p to 311p. Thus taking the value of 2393p on 23 February 2009, the probable price range five trading days into the future (2 March 2009) is from 2095p to 2704p. For comparison, the actual distribution of 5-day changes in AstraZeneca is shown in Figure 5.4. In this case the 95% probable price change is from -127p to 146p. A better comparison between these two methods is obtained by calculating the 95% probable price range by each method up to nine days into the future. This is shown in Table 5.1.

Table 5.1 – Comparison of the 95% probable price range for AstraZeneca price from one to nine days forward. The starting price on 23 February 2009 was 2393p. The column headed Millard is from the actual distribution, and the column headed Millard M.C. is from a simulation with 2000 trials.

Days forward	Millard low	Millard high	Millard M.C. low	Millard M.C. high
1	2334	2455	2334	2455
2	2311	2489	2274	2517
3	2296	2505	2214	2580
4	2270	2518	2155	2642
5	2266	2539	2095	2704
6	2245	2549	2035	2767
7	2235	2562	1975	2829
8	2216	2576	1916	2892
9	2215	2582	1856	2924

Figure 5.3 – The distribution of five-day changes in AstraZeneca from a Monte Carlo simulation using 2000 trials.

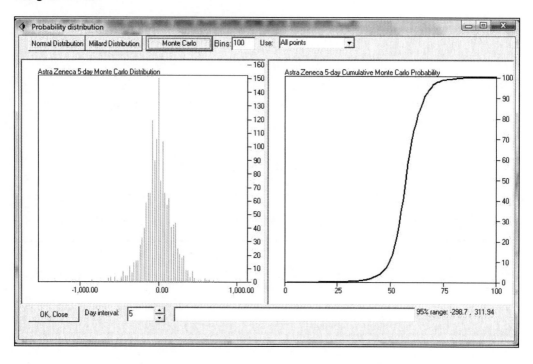

Figure 5.4 – The actual distribution of five-day changes in AstraZeneca.

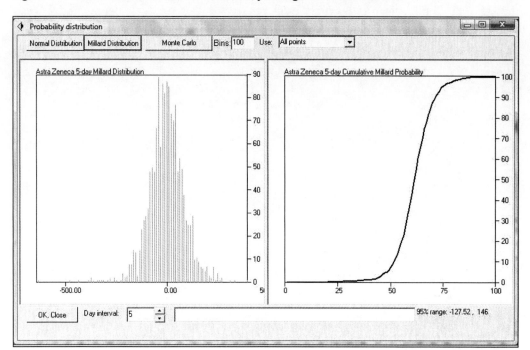

Table 5.2 – The movement of AstraZeneca nine days forward from 23 February 2009.

Date	Days forward	Close
23/02/09	0	2393
24/02/09	1	2415
25/02/09	2	2400
26/02/09	3	2357
27/02/09	4	2243
02/03/09	5	2240
03/03/09	6	2238
04/03/09	7	2213
05/03/09	8	2183
06/03/09	9	2147

Figure 5.5 – The data from Table 5.1 are now plotted. The solid line is the actual movement of the AstraZeneca price since 23 February 2009. The dotted lines are the upper and lower limits of the 95% probable price range from the Millard distribution. The dashed lines are those derived from a Millard version of the Monte Carlo simulation. Day one is the starting day on 23 February.

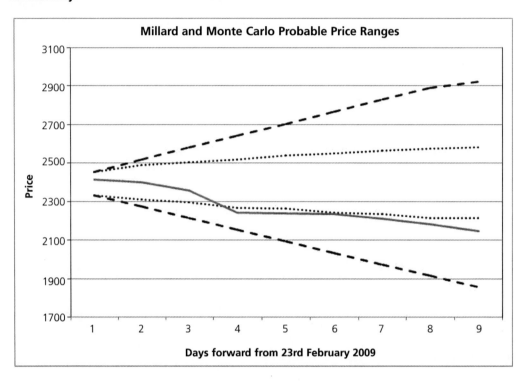

An examination of Figure 5.6 is very informative. We can see that using the 95% probabilities derived from the Millard distribution as described in the last chapter gives limits which are valid up to and including day four. However, after that the actual price falls below the lower limit and remains there to the last day (day 10 on the chart). The Monte Carlo 95% probabilities are valid throughout the chart, since the price remains comfortably within these limits, shown as a dashed line in the figure.

From these two different approaches to the calculation of the 95% probability range for future price movement, it can be seen that for the first four days, the Millard distribution method gives a tighter range for the predicted price and therefore is to be preferred. For longer periods into the future, the Millard version of the Monte Carlo simulation is to be preferred, even though it appears to give quite a wide range. We will see shortly how to address this issue of a wide range.

Figure 5.6 – The distribution of five-day changes in American Express from a Monte Carlo simulation using 2000 trials.

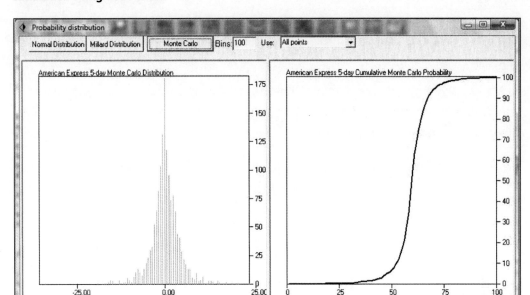

Just to confirm that these methods are applicable to other markets; in Figure 5.7 we show the Monte Carlo distribution of American Express. As was shown for AstraZeneca, the probability ranges derived from both the Millard distribution and the Monte Carlo simulations are shown in Table 5.3 for nine days forward.

Table 5.3 – Comparison of the 95% probable range for American Express price from one to nine days forward. The starting price on 6 March 2009 was $10.26. The column headed Millard is from the actual distribution and the column headed Millard M.C. is from a simulation with 2000 trials.

Days forward	Millard low	Millard high	Millard M.C. low	Millard M.C. high
1	8.89	11.56	8.89	11.56
2	8.4	12.26	7.52	12.87
3	7.9	12.33	6.15	14.18
4	7.74	12.66	4.78	15.48
5	7.39	12.86	3.86	16.79
6	7.15	13	2.39	18.1
7	6.67	13.12	0.68	19.41
8	6.53	12.92	0	20.71
9	6.46	13.3	0	22.02

The data from Table 5.3 are plotted in Figure 5.7. Since the calculation of probable price ranges for the Millard version of the Monte Carlo method gives negative results for eight and nine days forward, these are replaced with a zero value. Unless American Express goes bankrupt, zero values have no meaning, but are used here to give a lower limit which can be plotted.

Again, we see that the actual price movement violates the probabilities derived from the Millard distribution at day five. The probabilities derived from the Monte Carlo simulation remain valid across the whole nine days.

Figure 5.7 – The data from Table 5.3 are now plotted. The solid line is the actual movement of the American Express price since 6 March 2009. The dotted lines are the upper and lower limits of the 95% probable price range from the Millard distribution. The dashed lines are those derived from a Millard version of the Monte Carlo simulation.

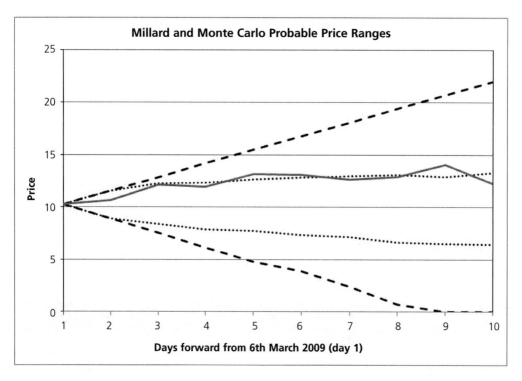

Narrowing the probability band

Using the 95% probability bands obviously gives a wide range for the predicted future price movement that limits the usefulness of the method. A way of reducing this range is to use a lower probability, for example 90%. This had been done for AstraZeneca as shown in Figure 5.8. Quite clearly the dashed lines for the Millard version of the Monte Carlo simulation are now much closer together. Although the price level gets close to the predicted lower 90% level at day five (four days into the future), it is still contained between the predicted high and low 90% probability levels throughout the period shown in Figure 5.8.

Figure 5.8 – The probability level for AstraZeneca has now been reduced to 90%. The solid line is the actual movement of the AstraZeneca price since 23 February 2009. The dotted lines are the upper and lower limits of the 95% probable price range from the Millard distribution. The dashed lines are those derived from a Millard version of the Monte Carlo simulation. Day one is the starting day on 23 February. The dashed lines are now closer together compared with those for 95% probabilities shown in Figure 5.5.

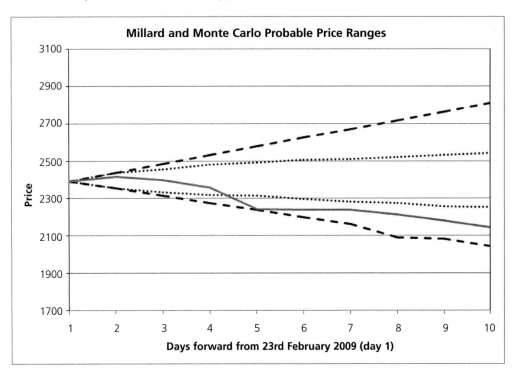

When drawing these levels on a chart in order to predict future price movement, it is best to draw a vertical line at the appropriate point in time which covers the predicted range. As an example, the predicted price range for AstraZeneca nine days into the future from the data point at 23 February 2009 is shown in Figure 5.9.

Figure 5.9 – The predicted price range nine days into the future from the latest data point on 23 February 2009 is shown as a vertical line.

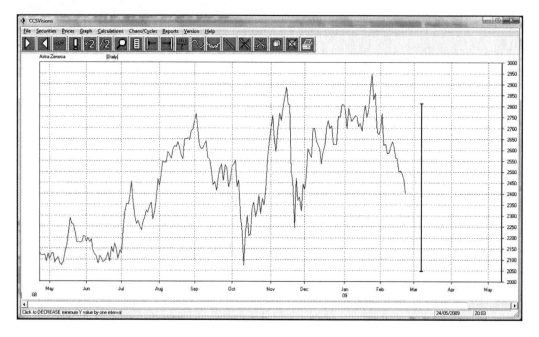

If intuition is brought to bear on the situation shown in Figure 5.9, then it would seem that the predicted price range is ridiculously large for a point in time only nine days into the future. The price range is from 2046 to 2811, which is a range of 765p. This is 32% of the latest price value at 2393p. However, this is a case where intuition is totally wrong, as shown in Figure 5.10, where the subsequent price movement is shown. It can be seen that the price fell over the next nine days by a large amount to a value of 2147p, only 100p above the lower value of the predicted range.

Figure 5.10 – Nine days into the future and the AstraZeneca price has fallen to a point not far above the low point of the predicted price range. The starting point on 23 February is indicated by the arrow.

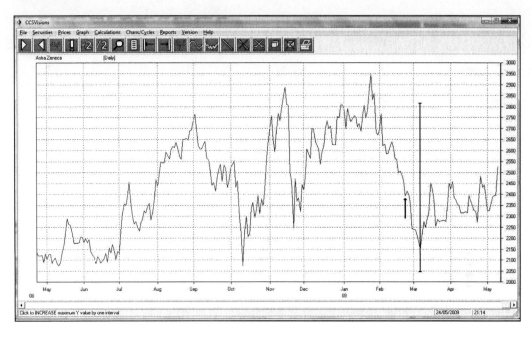

In order to reduce the predicted price range so that this low price of 2147p is close to the lower end of the predicted price range at day nine, the probability level would have to be reduced to 85%. This would give a predicted range of 2143p to 2715p.

It would be wrong to reduce the probability level to 85% and take this as a universally useful value, since this would be based on just this one example. In order to remain as a reliable method, it is best to use a probability level of 90% until future research shows that a better level is available.

What has been described in this chapter is another tool to use to examine probable price movement in the future. It is not intended to be a stand-alone method of prediction, but rather as part of the overall analysis of an individual stock which should always take place before a trading decision is taken.

6

Cycles and the Market

A cycle is a series of repeating events; there are many mathematical curves which exhibit this behaviour. Thus a particular section of the graph of such a curve can be seen as a pattern which is then repeated many times. For example, a cycloid is the curve formed by the vertical position of a point on a circle which is rolling on a flat surface. There are a number of interesting facts about a cycloid, such as the fact that the area under the curve is three times the area of the circle which generates it. Also the length of the cycloid is four times the diameter of the generating circle. An example of a repeating cycloid is shown in Figure 6.1.

Figure 6.1 – A cycloid such as that shown here is formed by a point on the circumference of a rolling circle.

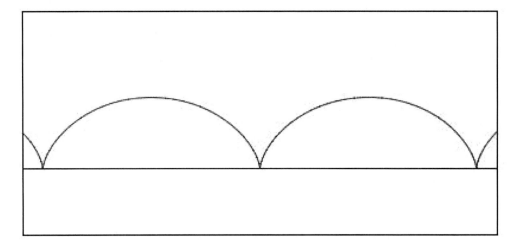

It is possible to find this type of curve in market data, but the pattern does not repeat more than once. Usually such a pattern in the market is characterised by an increasing rate of fall to a point from which it rises equally rapidly. An example is shown in Figure 6.2.

Figure 6.2 – This short section of the closing values of the Honeywell stock price shows some characteristics of a cycloid with rounded tops and a sharp reversal from its lows.

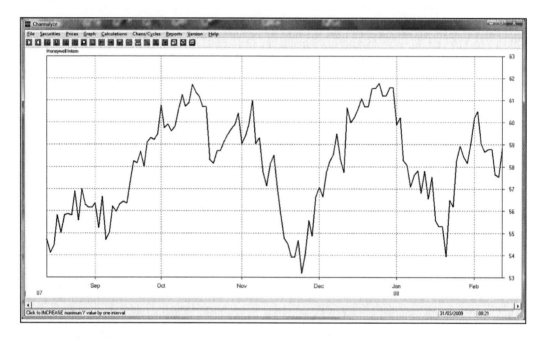

However, owing to its infrequent occurrence, the cycloid is of no significance in helping us to predict market movement in a more general sense. Of much more interest to us is the sine curve, an example of which is shown in Figure 6.3.

Figure 6.3 – A sine wave.

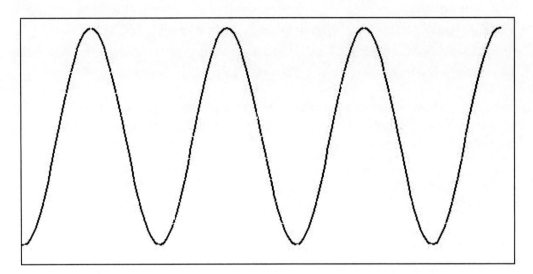

We will be able to demonstrate that the cycles which are present in market data are indeed of this type.

Properties of Sine Waves

Sine waves such as that shown in Figure 6.3 are completely defined if we know three variables. These are:

- Wavelength or frequency

- Amplitude

- Phase

To help in future discussion we will define the section, from one point on the wave to the next corresponding point, as a sweep.

Wavelength

The wavelength is the distance between any point on the wave to the next corresponding point. For ease of measurement, this can be taken as the distance from one trough to the next trough or one peak to the next peak. A sweep therefore covers one wavelength.

Wavelengths in the stock market are expressed in minutes, days, weeks or years. As far as this book is concerned, we will be using days, since we will only be concerned with daily closing values. We will not be using intra-day data, so that wavelengths in minutes will not be applicable. Two sine waves with different wavelengths but similar amplitudes are shown in Figure 6.4. One wavelength is three times the other.

Figure 6.4 – This shows two sine waves of different wavelengths. One wavelength (thin line) is three times that of the other (thicker line). The sine wave of shorter wavelength terminates short of the right-hand edge.

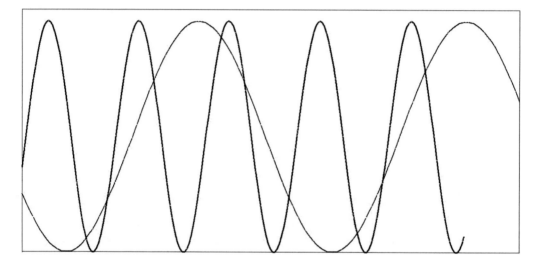

Frequencies are inversely related to wavelengths. Thus a wavelength of 10 days is equivalent to a frequency of 0.1 per day. A frequency of 50 days is equivalent to a frequency of 0.02 per day.

Amplitude

For our purposes we will take the amplitude of a sine wave to be the vertical distance from trough to peak. For stock market data this may be measured in a unit of currency, i.e. UK pounds/pence or US dollars/cents. For indices the measurement is simply a number, while for currencies it is of course a number which represents a ratio. A plot of two sine waves with the same wavelength but different amplitudes is shown in Figure 6.5. Since the wavelengths are the same and the phase is the same the peaks and troughs occur at the same positions.

Figure 6.5 – This shows two sine waves of the same wavelength but different amplitudes. The phase of each is identical.

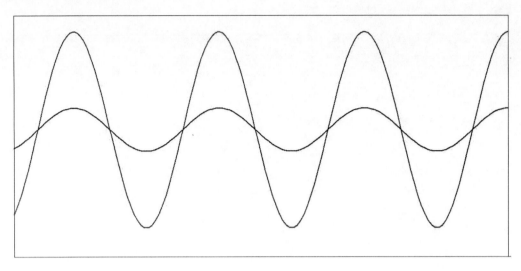

Phase

The phase is a more difficult concept, but it represents how far the sine wave is from some arbitrary starting point. The only way that this can be checked is to use a particular feature such as a peak, trough or mid-point.

Thus two sine waves can look exactly the same, but when plotted on the same chart the difference is obvious. This is shown in Figure 6.6, where two sine waves are superimposed. They both have a wavelength of 41 days, which can be verified by checking the position of the peaks and troughs in each wave.

Figure 6.6 – This shows two sine waves out of phase by half a wavelength. One has peaks at 1108, 1149 and 1190. The other has peaks at 1128 and 1169. The wavelength of both is 41 days and the amplitudes are identical.

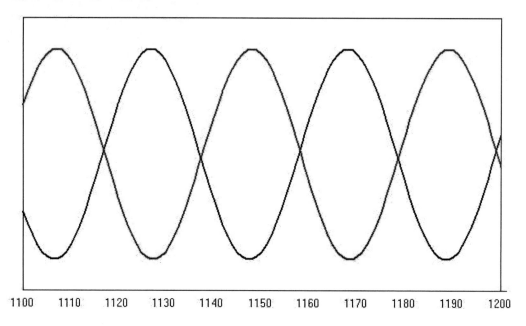

It can be seen that both of the sine waves also have the same amplitude.

The fact that they are exactly half a wavelength out of phase means that the peak of one is at the same position as the trough of the other. If the phase difference increases then the peaks (and troughs) of the two waves will separate even more. Of course, when the phases differ by an exact multiple of the wavelength, the peaks and troughs will coincide again. In such a case the two waves are essentially the same.

Harmonics

This is the term used to describe those frequencies which are an exact multiple of the original frequency. Thus the second harmonic has twice the frequency of the original, the third harmonic three times the frequency of the original, and so on.

Since wavelength is the inverse of the frequency, the second harmonic will be half of the wavelength of the original, the third harmonic one-third of the wavelength of the original and so on. The amplitude of the harmonics decrease as we move from second to third and so on. This decrease in amplitude as we move to shorter wavelengths is a fundamental property that will have implications for the relationship between the amplitudes of cycles of different wavelength in the same security.

Harmonics are mentioned here because it is quite possible that they exist in the cycles in market data. As will be shown later, many cycles are related by such a multiple. They also pass the test for change in amplitude.

Equation of a sine wave

Now we know the three variables that make up a sine wave, we can put them together in the form of an equation relevant to the stock, foreign exchange or commodities markets.

This equation takes the following form:

```
Y = amplitude x sin (F + W x t)
```

Where:

```
Y = value in currency, index points, etc.

W = 2 x Pi/N

N = wavelength

Pi = 3.142

t = time in same units as N

F = a measurement of phase as discussed earlier.
```

Therefore in order to find the value for Y at some time (t) in the future for a given sine wave, we simply need to establish the wavelength (N), the amplitude and the phase.

If we have a section of sine wave sufficient to give us values for amplitude and wavelength we can calculate the equation which describes it. We can then plot the future path of this sine wave. We can adjust the phase until the calculated extension to the existing sine wave has a maximum or minimum exactly one wavelength forward from the last true maximum or minimum. The result of doing this is shown in Figure 6.7.

Figure 6.7 – Once the wavelength and amplitude of the sine wave (solid line) are known, then its equation can be derived. It can then be extrapolated into the future (broken line).

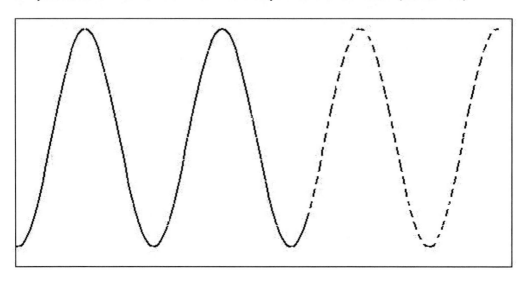

At this point we have covered the theory behind sine waves which can be derived mathematically. These sine waves are of course regular in the sense that the wavelength, amplitude and phase remain constant. This is why we can extrapolate any such sine wave into the future.

Cycles in the Stock Market

When we look at waves that are present in the stock market, we will not see such regularity. We will find that each of the three components (wavelength, amplitude and phase) will not remain constant but will vary over the course of the evolution of the price data.

Nominal wavelength

Since all three of the components of a sine wave in the market can change, it could be argued, philosophically, that the change in one or more components means that we are no longer observing the same sine wave. However, it helps the discussion to take the view that we can accept variations in the three components of a sine wave and consider it to be the same wave, as long as these variations are limited in nature. The way to do this is to use the term 'nominal wavelength' to describe its average wavelength, around which limited change is allowable. We could also take the view that since a change in phase would shift the position of peaks and troughs from their originally estimated position, then an apparent change in wavelength may not be an actual change in wavelength but a change in phase. However, the cause of an apparent change in wavelength is immaterial; it is the fact of a change that is important.

This can be demonstrated by isolating a cycle of nominal wavelength by the methods discussed in later chapters; such a plot is shown in Figure 6.8.

Figure 6.8 – The cycle of nominal wavelength 130 days in the Tesco stock price (lower panel). It can be seen that the amplitude and wavelength are changing. The lumpy appearance is due to the influence of cycles of shorter wavelength. The stock price is shown in the upper panel.

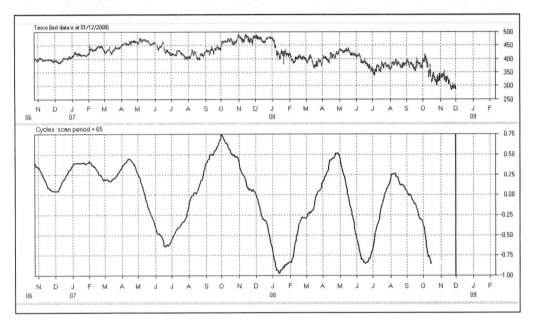

This shows quite clearly the variation in amplitude and wavelength of a cycle with a nominal wavelength of 130 days. The term 'nominal' is used here because this is the average wavelength around which the increase and decrease is occurring. Quite clearly the two peaks at October 07 and May 08 are further apart than the peaks at May 08 and August 08. It can also be seen that the amplitude is decreasing gradually.

Working backwards, from right to left, a peak around February 2007 would have been expected if this gap between peaks was to be maintained. However, on inspection, it can be seen that the peak has been distorted by the addition of a cycle of much shorter wavelength, which is bottoming out at almost the exact place where the nominal 130-day cycle would have been topping out.

A much better appreciation of the variation in wavelength and amplitude can be seen from Figure 6.9. Here a longer history of the cycles can be seen. The time axis is now shown in days rather than dates. In this mode it is easier to establish the distance apart of peaks and troughs.

Figure 6.9 – A longer section of cycles is shown here (lower panel) which highlights the more extreme changes in amplitude and wavelength which can occur. The stock price is shown in the upper panel.

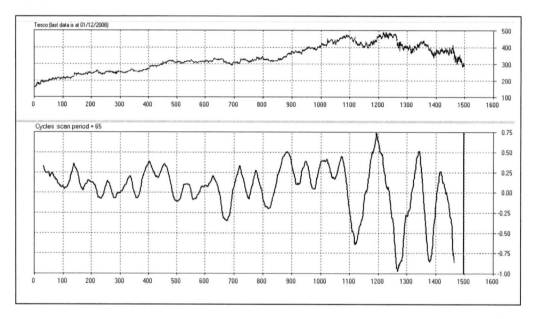

From the appearance of Figures 6.8 and 6.9 it might well be thought that using cycles in market data to predict future movement is fraught with such difficulty that it is not worth the attempt. However, by using better mathematics than used to produce Figures 6.8 and 6.9, the result shown in Figure 6.10 was obtained. Here there is a much smoother trace for the cycle. Because of that smoothness, the cycle produced by this method, although still varying in amplitude and wavelength at the right-hand section of the plot, shows a much less marked change.

Figure 6.10 – The nominal cycle of wavelength 113 days in American Express (lower panel). The last half of a wavelength (broken line) has been extrapolated. The stock price is shown in the upper panel.

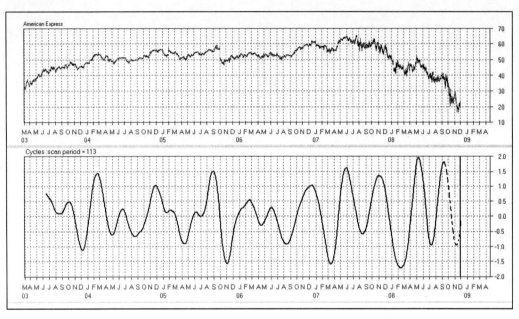

Note that the last half of a wavelength of the cycle is shown as a broken line. This is to show that this is an extrapolation from the last true calculated point, which terminates about half a wavelength back in time from the latest data point. The reason for this is explained in a later chapter.

The extrapolation is carried out by taking an average of the wavelength and amplitude over the last few sweeps of the cycle to calculate the equation of the equivalent sine wave. As will be seen later, such an extrapolation is only valid where the last few sweeps of a cycle fall within specified limits (e.g. 20%) of variation in both wavelength and amplitude.

The correctness of the extrapolation of this nominal 113-day cycle can be seen in Figure 6.11, where the data was taken several months later. The actual downward leg of the cycle agrees exactly with the predicted path from the earlier extrapolation.

Figure 6.11 – Several months later, it can be seen that the extrapolation was exactly correct. The downward leg of the cycle agrees with the predicted position from Figure 6.10.

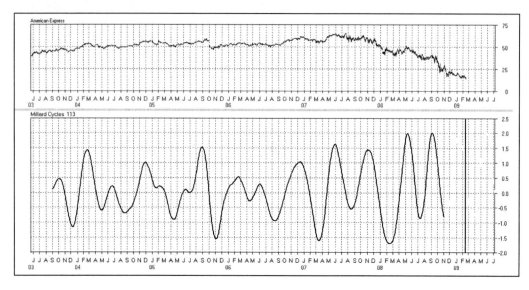

An example of a very regular cycle is found in the foreign exchange market in the Australian dollar versus the euro, as shown in Figure 6.12. The nominal wavelength in this case is 83 days. The most striking element of this chart is the regularity of wavelength. This stays within 20% across the whole plot.

Figure 6.12 – A plot of the Australian dollar versus the euro (upper panel). The cycle shown is the nominal 83-day cycle (lower panel).

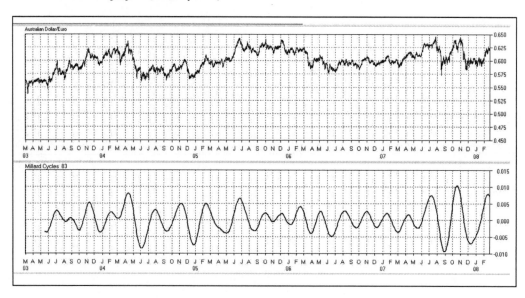

Thus in this case only the amplitude seems to vary to any great extent. Even so, from January 2006 to April 2007 the variation in amplitude was quite limited.

From these examples it can be seen that in many cases a cycle will pass through a state where it is relatively stable for a number of sweeps. During other time periods it is unstable in the sense that both the wavelength and the amplitude are varying by an amount which is outside the allowable limit of 20%.

In order to predict trends into the future, only cycles which have been in this relatively stable state over the last few complete sweeps can be used. The validity of this approach in the prediction of future trends will become apparent in later chapters, where predicted trends can be compared with actual trends. In some cases an extraordinary degree of prediction of trends will be evident.

Research on Market Cycles

The existence of cycles in the market has of course been known for a long time. Thus there is the four-year presidential cycle in the United States, there is the Halloween indicator, in which it appears that buying around Halloween time and selling in May is more often profitable than not and so on.

In my book *Channel Analysis*, published in 1990 and reissued in 2009, I listed the known cycles in stock market data. This was based upon the work of many analysts throughout the last century.

Table 6.1 – Known cycles in stock market data.

Years	Months	Weeks	Days*	Relative amplitude
54				150
36				132
16				117.1
9.5				95.8
9.2				93.1
7.1				82.5
4.3	51	223		55.75
3.2	38	166		41.5
1.8	21	94		23.5
0.8	9.6	42		10.5
		33	165	8.25
		9	45	2.25
		7	35	1.75
		4	20	1

*days are business days, i.e. five per week.

The amplitudes of these various cycles appear to be directly proportional to the wavelength for the shorter-term cycles, but the increase tails off as we move to higher wavelengths.

The cycles of wavelength greater than 4.3 years are of no practical use to the trader.

It is interesting to note that J.M. Hurst gave a different set of cycles in his book *The Profit Magic of Stock Transaction Timing.*

Table 6.2 – Market cycles according to J.M. Hurst.

Years	Months	Weeks	Days
18			
9			
4.5			
3			
1.5	18		
0.75	12		
0.5	6	26	130
0.25	3	13	65
	1.5	6.5	32
	0.75	3.25	16
	0.38	1.63	8

Hurst stated quite categorically that under what he called the Commonality Principle these cyclic components were present in all securities.

In my research on those cycles that are stable over the last few sweeps I have arrived at a different conclusion from those which are illustrated in these two tables. In both the US and UK markets there seems to be very little correlation between stable cycles in individual securities. This is also true of the foreign exchange markets.

Of course, finding that at the time this book was being written (January to June 2009) there is no correlation does not mean that there was no such correlation in the past. Naturally the observation that cycles spend most of their history in a state of instability means that it makes sense that there is very little correlation, since an exact wavelength cannot be put on an unstable cycle.

Thus each individual security must have the wavelengths of its own cycles established and from this its own future trend determined without reference to any other security, other than, as discussed in Chapter 2, a consideration of the overall state of the market.

Coincidence of cycle peaks or troughs

When two or more cycles with different wavelengths are present and they happen to coincide in the position of a peak or trough, then the question arises as to how far into the future this will happen again. This depends entirely upon the wavelengths involved. The problem is solved by using the method for finding the lowest common multiple of the cycles. Take the case of two cycles with wavelengths, say, 20 days and 75 days that have coincident peaks today. We list multiples of each by multiplying each by 2, 3, 4, 5 and so on. We will get:

20, 40, 60, 80, 100, 120, 140, 160, 180, 200, 220, 240, 260, 280, 300

75, 150, 225, 300

From this we can see that the first common multiple is the value of 300. This means that the peaks will be only coincident again 300 days from now. During that time, the cycle of wavelength 20 will have seen 15 peaks and the cycle of wavelength 75 will have seen four peaks.

Unfortunately, because of the variation in wavelength in market cycles, this coincidence will be difficult to predict with any certainty.

7

Trends and the Market

The *Oxford English Dictionary* defines a trend as "general direction and tendency". Wikipedia, that rather less authoritative but more popular source of information, defines a market trend as "a prolonged period of time when prices in a financial market are rising or falling faster than their historical average, also known as 'bull' and 'bear' markets, respectively". What is meant by 'historical average' is not explained.

Wikipedia also defines trend estimation as "the statistical analysis of data to extrapolate trends". It goes on to further define a market trend in these terms: "this principle incorporates the idea that market cycles occur with regularity and persistence. This belief is considered to be generally consistent with the practice of technical analysis". Note the use of 'trend' and 'cycles' in the same definition.

In this book we will not consider the traditional way of presenting uptrends and downtrends, as shown in Figure 7.1, to be representative of trends in the sense that we shall be using throughout this book.

Figure 7.1 – The traditional way of showing uptrends and downtrends is shown by the lines on this chart.

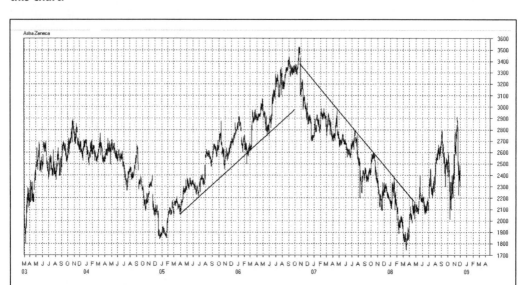

There are two main reasons for not proceeding any further with the traditional way of drawing trends as exemplified by Figure 7.1.

These are:

1. Trends drawn in this way do not satisfy the requirements of a mathematical trend.

2. There are no numbers upon which mathematical and statistical calculations can be performed which can lead to probabilities.

Mathematical Trends

By 'mathematical trends' we mean trends that are derived from a mathematical formula, such as a straight line, a polynomial, etc. In other words the trend is represented by a mathematical equation. On the other hand the straight lines shown in Figure 7.1, like any other straight lines, have intrinsic equations to describe them, but since they have been drawn on the chart using a ruler or its equivalent, these are not immediately known. It is not necessary for the reader to worry about the way in which such trends are calculated, since spreadsheet programs will do this. In the case of moving averages, all technical analysis software packages are able to carry out such a calculation. However, users of moving averages might not be aware that a moving average represents a trend, as discussed later.

Straight line

A straight-line trend is shown in Figure 7.2. This is calculated on the closing prices over 100 days of the London Stock Exchange. The major way in which this straight line differs from those shown in Figure 7.1 is that the data oscillates around the line, i.e. some data points appear above the line and others below the line. This is a fundamental property of trends calculated in this way and is the reason that in this book it is this fundamental type of trend with which we will be concerned.

Figure 7.2 – This shows a straight-line trend drawn on the closing prices of the London Stock Exchange. The chart has been produced by the Excel spreadsheet program.

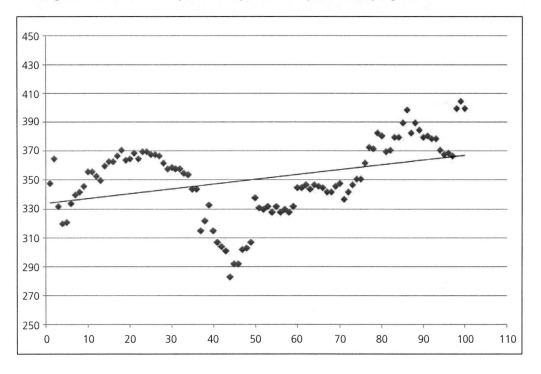

Since the trend is based on the known equation of a straight line, then obviously it can be projected into the future.

Whether the future trend can still be represented by this straight line is a different matter and the point at which this straight line fails to represent the trend of the data is not known in advance. However, various statistical tests can be applied, as each new data point arrives, that can help to determine whether or not the straight trend line for the new data is still valid.

Polynomial

There are many other types of trend lines that can be applied to the data, for example a polynomial. The variable in this case is the order of the polynomial. Thus in Figure 7.3 we show a second order polynomial trend line (quadratic) drawn through the same data. Again we see the fundamental property that the data lies above and below the trend line. But, as is the case with the straight line, the quadratic equation of this line is known and therefore it can be projected into the future. As with the straight line, whether or not the trend line is still valid for future data points cannot be determined in advance.

Figure 7.3 – A quadratic trend line has been drawn (using Excel) through the same set of data as that used in Figure 7.2.

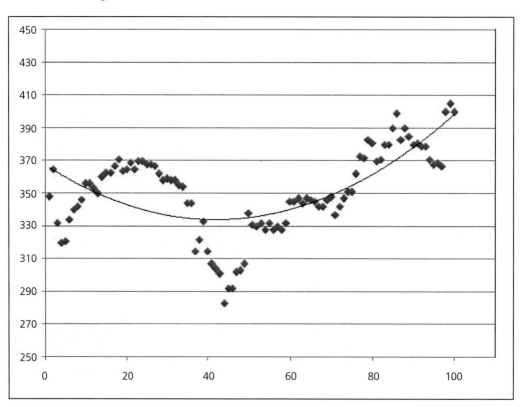

Change in trend line

It must be clearly understood that a trend line calculated from a data set will almost certainly not be the same as a trend line calculated from a portion of that data set. This can be seen in Figure 7.4, where only the first 50 points of the London Stock Exchange data have been used to calculate a quadratic trend line. Quite obviously this line does not marry up with the longer line which was plotted in Figure 7.3.

Figure 7.4 – A quadratic trend line has now been drawn through the first 50 points of the data used in Figure 7.3.

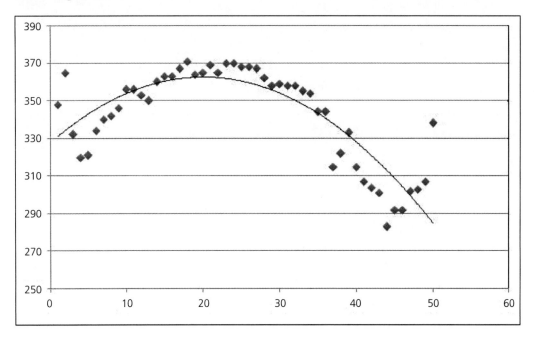

Change with one data point

As a new data point arrives, the only way in which the trend line will remain the same is if the new data point lies on the trend line. Any other position for the new data point will change the equation of the trend line and hence its position.

Change with several data points

Although the only way the equation of the line can remain the same is if the first new data point lies on it, this does not imply that the only way for a trend line to remain valid will be if all subsequent points to arrive also lie on the line.

> **"** The only way in which the trend line will remain the same is if the new data point lies on the trend line. **"**

If the first new point does not lie on the line, then the next point to arrive must lie on the other side of the projected trend line if there is to be no change from the original trend. Not only that, but there will be only one position for this new point that will result in the recalculated trend being the same as the original. In the case of market data this is of course unlikely.

Once a number of new points have arrived then a recalculation may well result in the equation of the new line being the same as that of the original. Again, this is unlikely in the case of market data, although there might not be a large change.

It has to be accepted therefore that predicted trends in market data will change as new data points arrive. This is why it is extremely important that trends are recalculated each day. If the recalculated trend lies within the expected range then all is well. If not – if the trend is seen to move in the wrong direction – then action must be taken.

The sequence of Figures 7.5 to 7.7 shows the effect that each new data point has on the quadratic trend which was drawn on the chart in Figure 7.4. A careful inspection of the position of this trend line relative to the last six points shows that it is gradually moving higher as each new point is added to the data set. This is of course because each new point is lying at a higher value than the last calculated value of the trend line.

> **"** It is extremely important that trends are recalculated each day. **"**

Figures 7.5 to 7.7 – Note the small change in the latest position of the trend.

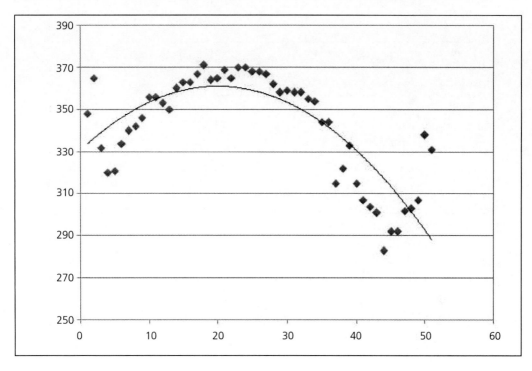

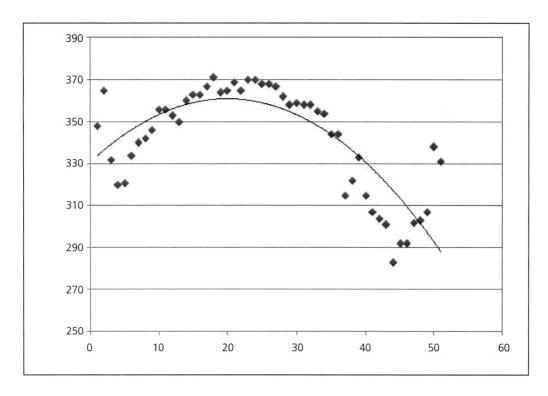

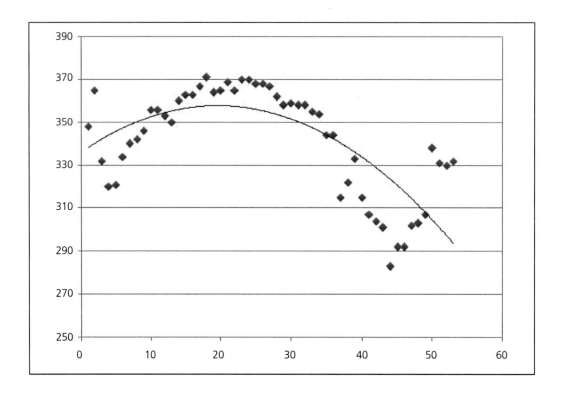

Goodness of fit

So far we have used two distinct types of trend lines – straight lines and quadratic lines. The simple way in which to tell if these are reasonable representations of the trend in the data is to apply a statistical calculation. This is a huge topic and those interested may of course search for more information on the internet. A useful website can be found at: www.curvefit.com.

One method is to use a quantity known as R^2. This quantity lies between 0 and 1.0. The higher the value, the better is the fit of the line to the data from which it is derived. A value of 1.0 can only be obtained if all of the data points lie on the line – this will never happen with stock market data. A value of 0 means that there is no fit, with a horizontal line placed at the average Y value for the data being just as meaningful.

The quantity R^2 is calculated from the squares of the vertical distances of the data point from the line. Squares are used so that negative distances will be equally as important as positive distances.

This book is not intended to delve too much into the realm of this type of statistics. I am simply pointing out that computing trend lines is not a haphazard process, but that there are mathematical processes underlying the calculations to give confidence that the approach is correct.

When using a spreadsheet such as Excel to produce a trend line the value for R^2 is calculated for you and can be displayed if required. Thus for the quadratic trend lines shown in Figures 7.5 to 7.7, the values for R^2 are 0.699, 0.631 and 0.575 respectively. Clearly in this particular instance the quadratic is not a good trend line. It was only used here as an example to show the effect of the arrival of new points on the overall calculation.

Moving averages

Another form of trend line is that produced by using moving averages. The variable in this case is the period used for the average. There are also various ways of plotting such averages. They can be plotted with no lag, or with a lag which is usually half of the period used. In this case the averages are termed centred. This type of average will be used exclusively in this book except in this current section, where un-lagged averages are used to illustrate this same issue of change of trend line as each new data point arrives.

Figure 7.8 shows a five-point moving average of the same set of data from the London Stock Exchange that was used for the previous examples. Note how much more responsive the average is to the position of the last few data points compared to the quadratic trend line.

Figure 7.8 – A five-point moving average of 50 points of the London Stock Exchange data.

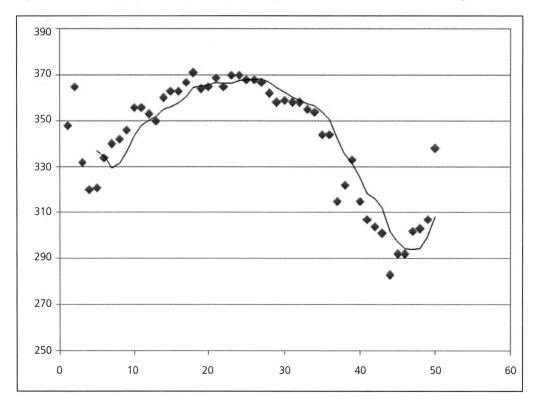

Shown in Figures 7.9 to 7.11 is the change in the plot of the average as new points arrive. Although only slight, there is a fall-off in the rate at which the average is rising.

Figures 7.9 to 7.11 – Note the small change in the latest position of the trend line.

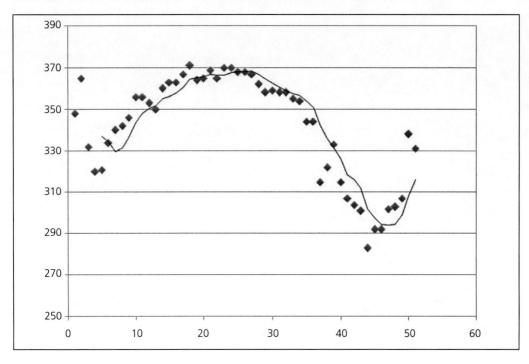

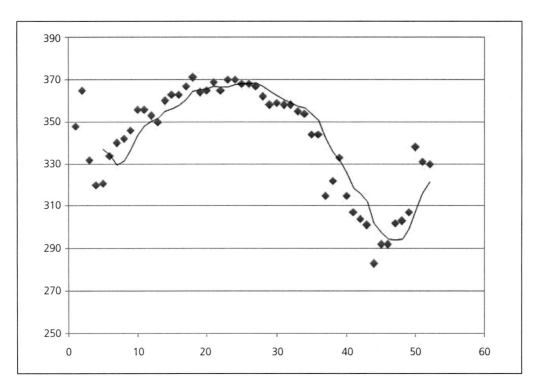

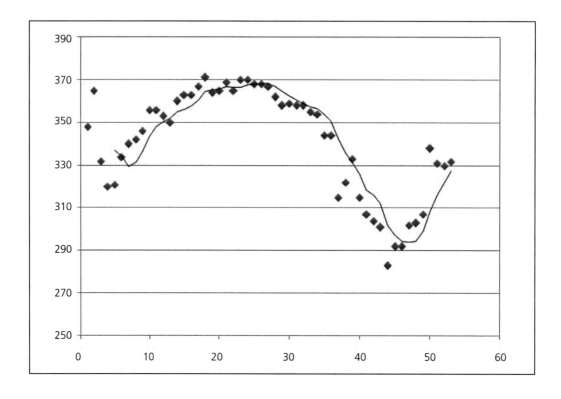

What *moving* means

There is a major difference between the way in which straight trend lines and quadratic trend lines are calculated compared with moving averages. In the case of the former, all of the data points were used in the calculation. Thus as new points arrive they have an influence on the whole of the plotted trend line.

On the other hand, moving averages use only the last n points in the calculation (where n is the period used for the average).

Starting from the beginning of the data, the first n points are used to calculate the first value. This sum is then divided by n to bring the resulting value to a similar order as the original data.

The calculation then shifts one point forwards and the first n points from this position are used to calculate the next value for the average. Thus the calculation moves forward through the data one point at a time, which is the reason for the term 'moving'.

Because only the last n points are used to calculate the final value there will be no change in the position or shape of the average over the points prior to these final n

points. In other words a new point only has influence on the *n* points of which it is the final point.

Figure 7.12 – A plot where a 25-point moving average has been used.

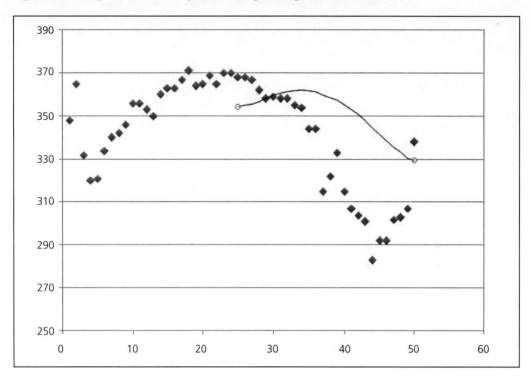

Naturally, the larger we make n, the further back the influence of the new point extends. However, on the other hand, its influence gets smaller because the sum of the *n* points is then divided by n. These issues will be discussed in more detail in the next chapter.

Extrapolating a trend line

Linear and polynomial

Although moving averages are the key to prediction of future trends, as we shall see later in this book, there is a major difficulty in extrapolating them into the future. Linear trend lines and polynomial trend lines are characterised by an algebraic equation. Putting on one side the question of whether or not the trend line will be valid into the future, it is this equation which can be used to determine its future position. As we have discussed, although each new datum has the potential to change the trend, at any given time there is a mathematical basis for assuming that the trend will continue into the future and as such can be used as a predictor.

Moving averages

Unfortunately there is no underlying equation associated with a moving average line. Thus it cannot be projected accurately into the future by simple mathematics. We can use the moving average's current rate of curvature to project it into the future, but as we will see later this is subject to huge error at those points where a trend is changing direction.

We will show in later chapters that we can extrapolate a moving average trend line by three methods – using probable future movement derived from distributions, using channel analysis, and, the most fundamental of these three methods, using studies of stable cycles and their sums.

Timescale of trends

It is obvious that the moving average shown in Figure 7.8 is quite different from the moving average shown in Figure 7.12. Thus, the fact of using two different periods for the averages has resulted in the isolation of two different trends from the same data.

This concept, that there can be a number of trends co-existing within the same set of market data, is a vital one, since it will lead to an understanding of how stock prices move. Once this has been grasped, the process by which trends can be isolated and then predicted becomes clear.

As far as the stock market is concerned, for convenience we can divide trends into short term, medium term and long term.

According to Wikipedia, trends can be divided into primary, secondary and secular trends. However, it is clear that Wikipedia is applying these terms to an entire market. The secular trend is very long term and lasts from five to twenty-five years. The primary trends can last for a year or more. The secondary trend lasts for between a few weeks and a few months. According to Wikipedia the secondary trend acts in the opposite direction to the primary trend. I do not take this view, since the methods we will be using to isolate trends will make no distinction between rising trends and falling trends, but only between their timescales. It is perfectly possible to have two trends (of different timescales) both rising or both falling at the same time.

> " It is perfectly possible to have two trends (of different timescales) both rising or both falling at the same time. "

In this book we shall take long-term trends to be those which last for more than nine months, medium term between six weeks and nine months and short term one to six weeks. Expressed in days, therefore, long term is over 200 days, medium-term 30 to 200 days and short-term five to 30 days.

Since we will consider an uptrend to be the rising part of a cycle and a downtrend the falling part of a cycle, then obviously these categories of trend timescales are caused by cycles with wavelengths twice the time taken for the trend to rise or fall. Thus a short-term trend is caused by cycles of period 10 to 60 days, a medium-term trend by cycles of period 60 to 400 days and a long-term trend by cycles of period over 400 days. Trends which fall into these categories are shown in Figure 7.13.

Figure 7.13 – How trends can be categorised into long-term (A), medium-term (B) and short-term (C) trends.

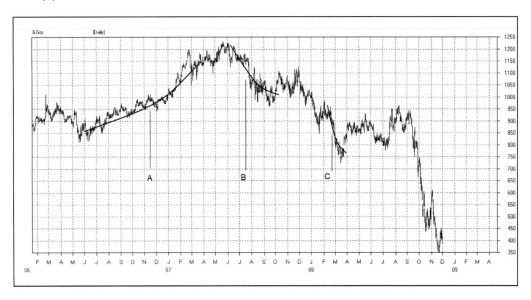

These are of course arbitrary distinctions, but they will serve us well when we come to decide how to isolate cycles or bands of cycles corresponding to these categories. Note the use of the term bands. Only rarely is a trend caused by just one cycle. There is usually a range or band of cycles which are responsible for a particular short-, medium- or long-term trend.

This will become obvious as we delve further into the relationship between cycles and trends in the following chapters.

8

Properties of Moving Averages

In this chapter we will be investigating the properties of moving averages and how they can be used to represent a trend in market data. We will also see the advantage in plotting centred averages rather than unlagged averages, which is the common way of presenting them on charts.

Calculation of Moving Averages

Since, as mentioned in the previous chapter, all technical analysis packages can calculate averages, it might appear to be unnecessary to show how they are calculated. However an appreciation of the process will serve us very well in investigating the properties of moving averages and will also show their value when used to investigate cycles.

We will take as an example a set of market data of which the first ten values are designated by V1, V2, V3, etc up to V10. Suppose that we also need to calculate a five-point average. We can designate the values for these averages as A5, A6, A7, etc up to A10. Note that we do not start with an A1, because the first average point is calculated by using the first five data points. Thus A5 is the value we calculate once we have reached point V5.

Once we have arrived at a total for the first five data points, we have to divide this total by five to arrive at a value for the average A5.

Thus:

$$A5 = (V1 + V2 + V3 + V4 + V5)/5$$

$$A6 = (V2 + V3 + V4 + V5 + V6)/5$$

$$A7 = (V3 + V4 + V5 + V6 + V7)/5$$

and so on up to the final point V10.

In general, therefore, to calculate an n-point average we would sum the first n points to arrive at a total and then divide this total by n. This gives us the first value for our average and using the nomenclature shown for the five-point average this first calculated point would be *An*.

They are arranged in this way to help to draw attention to an important aspect of the calculation. This is that, as we move the calculation onwards through the data, the last point of the five is dropped and the next point added in. Thus, whether the value for the average rises or falls when the next point is taken into consideration depends only upon the difference between the new point and the dropped point. If the new point has a higher value than the dropped point, the sum of the five points increases and so the new value of the average increases. Conversely, if the new point has a lower value than the dropped point, the new value of the average decreases.

> " Thus, whether the value for the average rises or falls when the next point is taken into consideration depends only upon the difference between the new point and the dropped point. "

This can be seen from Figure 8.1, where a nine-point average has been plotted over the data. The points from 248 to 256 have been added and divided by nine to produce the average value at point 256 (embedded in the smooth average line). The next calculation will drop the point at 248 (which has a high value) and add in the point at 257 (which has a low value). Thus the average calculated at point 257 will be lower than the value at point 256.

Figure 8.1 – This shows why the next calculated point of the nine-point average will be lower than the previous value. The new point has a lower value than the dropped point.

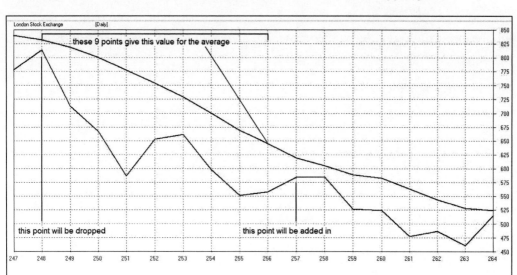

Of course, the average plotted in Figure 8.1 is plotted with no lag. Thus the average calculated using points 248 to 256 is plotted at the same position in time as point 256 and the next calculation of the average using point 257 is plotted at the same point in time as point 257.

From this the reader can see the fallacy in the way in which moving averages are used by many technical analysts. They use rules which are based on the general view that when the price rises above the average it is time to buy and when it falls below the average it is time to sell. However, as we have seen from the discussion of the dropped point, it is not whether the value of the data is higher than the current value of the average that causes the average to rise, but whether the value of the data is higher than the value of the dropped point.

Why does an average smooth the data?

The answer is because of the way it interacts with cyclic data. A moving average will totally or partially remove cycles from the data. We can divide this discussion into three parts:

1. there is the effect on cycles of the same wavelength as the period used for the average,

2. there is the effect on cycles of wavelength less than n, and

3. there is the effect on wavelengths greater than n.

Cycles with wavelength equal to period of the average

What happens here is that an average of period n will remove cycles with wavelength n. The reason for this is easy to explain in terms of the dropped point. This is shown in Figure 8.2.

Figure 8.2 – A cycle of wavelength 25. If the moving average has a period of 25, then each dropped point has the same value as the new point, as shown by the arrowed line. Thus the average remains at its first calculated value.

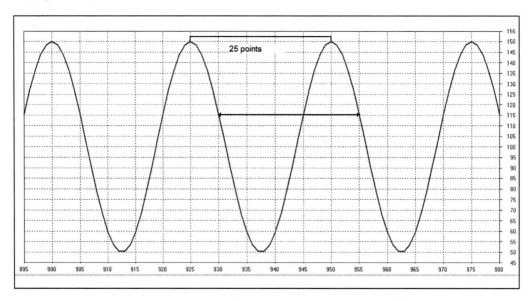

All points on the sine wave are identical in value to those points which are separated by one wavelength of 25. Because of this, every point which is dropped is replaced by a point of equal value. Thus the average remains at its first calculated value, producing a straight line, as shown in Figure 8.3.

Figure 8.3 – The result of applying a 25-point moving average to a cycle of wavelength 25 days. The output is a straight line for the reason shown in Figure 8.2.

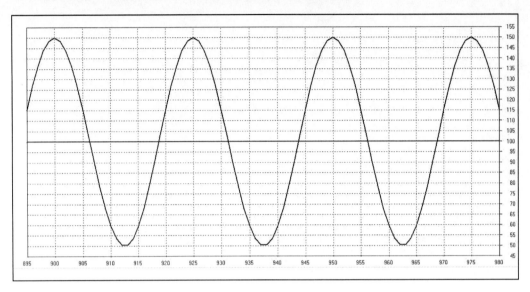

A moment's thought will lead you to the conclusion that cycles with wavelengths which are a multiple of the period used for the average will also be removed, since again every point that is dropped is replaced by a point of equal value.

Wavelengths higher than the average period

While cycles with wavelength equal to the period of the average are removed completely, cycles with wavelength higher than the period of the average are partially removed, i.e. attenuated. This attenuation decreases as the wavelength increases.

This can be seen in Figure 8.4. Here a cycle of wavelength 41 days has been produced. The output from the averages when applied to this cycle decreases in amplitude as we increase the period of the average, i.e. as the wavelength becomes higher relative to the period.

Figure 8.4 – The effect of applying nine-, 15- and 21-point averages to a cycle of wavelength 41 days. The closer the period of the average to the wavelength of the cycle, the greater is the attenuation.

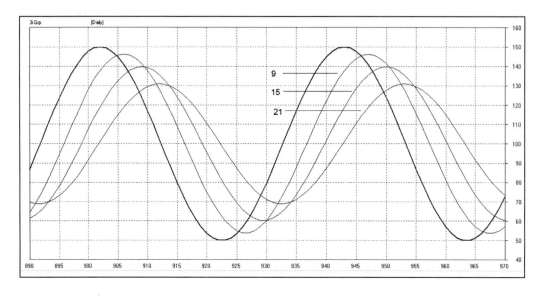

Wavelengths lower than the average period

While cycles with wavelength equal to the period of the average are removed completely, cycles with wavelength lower than the period of the average are partially removed, i.e. attenuated. This attenuation increases as the wavelength decreases.

Figure 8.5 – The effect of applying 31-, 39- and 41-point moving averages to a cycle of wavelength 41 days. The original cycle is the one with the maximum amplitude.

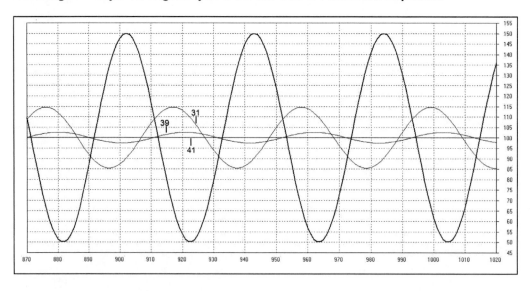

Centred averages

You will note in Figures 8.4 and 8.5 that the peaks and troughs in the output from applying moving averages to cycles do not align with the peaks and troughs in the original data. This is because the output has been plotted with no lag and therefore this means that the last calculated value for the average is plotted at the same point in time as the last data point. This is of course the traditional way used by technical analysts to plot averages.

We see also that the peaks and troughs in the output from each average do not line up with the individual peaks and troughs in the original data. There are many disadvantages in plotting averages in this way. The analysis of market data for cycles cannot be carried out and neither can any probabilities be derived.

To plot a centred average, it is necessary to understand that the latest value for the average must be plotted back in time from the latest data point. This offset is such as to plot the average value at the same position in time as that of the mid-point of the data points used to calculate that value of the average. In order that any point of the average coincides with a position in time of a data point, it is necessary to use an odd number for the periods. This will become clear if we now rewrite the formula used on page 92.

Now we change this so that A5 becomes A3, the centre point of the five data points used to calculate it. In other words, when we come to plot this average, the first calculated point, now designated A3, is to be plotted at the same position as data point three. It is important to understand that this does not affect the value of any of the points, simply how they are to be plotted.

Thus:

$$A3 = (V1 + V2 + V3 + V4 + V5)/5$$

$$A4 = (V2 + V3 + V4 + V5 + V6)/5$$

$$A5 = (V3 + V4 + V5 + V6 + V7)/5$$

and so on up to the final point V10.

When plotted in this way, the average of course terminates at a point in the past. The last plotted point will then be plotted at a position half of the span of the average back in time. Thus, we do not know how the average is likely to move over this gap between the position of the last calculated average point and the latest data point. This will not be known until we have moved that number of points which is equal to half a span of the average into the future. Then we will have enough future data points to be able to fill in the values across the gap.

Since in the next chapter we will be discussing using centred averages as proxies for trends, we will have to find ways of estimating how the average might move across this gap, what is its likely position at the present time, and what it is likely to do in the near future. It is this difficulty which will be explored in the next chapter.

When the averages which were plotted in Figure 8.4 are now plotted as centred averages, their peaks and troughs will now line up perfectly in time. The picture is now much more meaningful, as shown in Figure 8.6.

Figure 8.6 – When the nine-, 15- and 21-point centred averages are applied to the cycles of wavelength 41 days the peaks and troughs now line up perfectly.

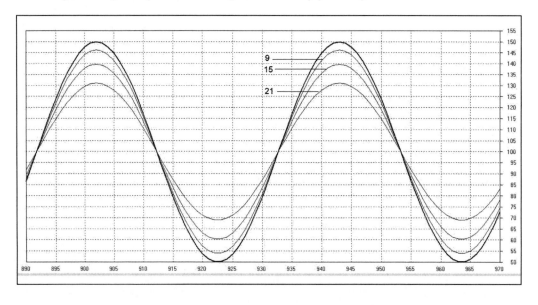

The effect of increased attenuation by averages as their period approaches the wavelength of the cycle is now much more obvious. The greater the wavelength of the cycle relative to the period of the average, the less is the attenuation. For wavelengths very much greater than the period used, the attenuation is almost negligible. This state of affairs is reached when the ratio of the wavelength to the period of the average exceeds about three. This is a very important point that we need to take into account later when isolating cycles by means of centred moving averages.

When the averages which were plotted in Figure 8.5 are now plotted as centred averages, once again the peaks and troughs line up perfectly. This is shown in Figure 8.7. Notice that, as in Figure 8.5, the effect of applying the 41-point average to the 41-day cycle is to completely remove it, leading to a straight line.

Figure 8.7 – When the 31-, 39- and 41-point centred averages are applied to a cycle of wavelength 41 days the peaks and troughs of the first two line up perfectly. The 41-point average has totally removed the cycle in its output, leading to a straight line. The closer the period of the average to the wavelength of the cycle, the greater is the attenuation.

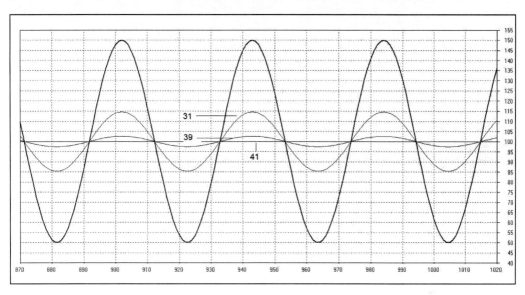

Applying averages to a mixture of cycles

Now we have seen the effect of applying moving averages of periods less than, equal to and greater than the wavelength of the cycle, it is important to examine how we can apply this knowledge to simple mixtures of cycles. This will enable us to arrive at the best ways of separating such cycles, so that we will be able to understand what happens when we use averages in an examination of real market data.

Three cycles of wavelength 41, 101 and 202 days with amplitudes of 25, 50 and 100 units respectively were combined with a horizontal straight line of 100 units. The plot of this complex waveform is shown in Figure 8.8.

Figure 8.8 – The plot of a sum of three cycles of wavelengths 41, 101 and 201 days and amplitudes 25, 50 and 100 points, with a straight line of value 100 points also added.

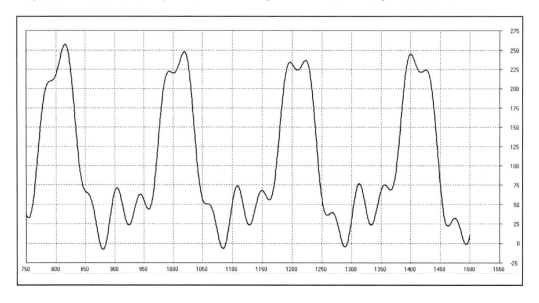

151-day average

If we were unaware of which cycles were present then we would have to test a few averages of different periods to form an idea of which cycles were present. A good starting point is a period of around half of the wavelength range of cycles in which we would be interested if examining the market. In this case we have applied a centred average of period 151 days. The result is shown in Figure 8.9

Figure 8.9 – A moving average of period 151 days has been applied to the data from Figure 8.8.

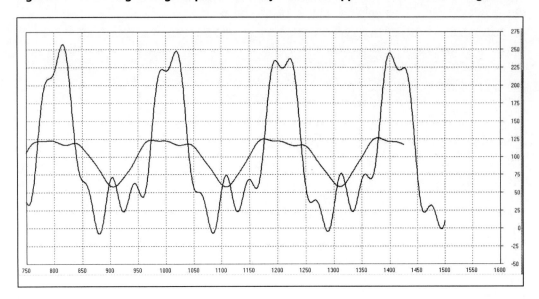

At this stage a great deal of information can be obtained. Firstly this average contains only a small amount of perturbation, so that we can take the distances between the clean troughs as being significant. These distances are 202 and 203. Thus we deduce that there is present a cycle of wavelength of around 202 or 203 days. Note that in a complex mixture these distances may be slightly distorted so that the wavelength deduced from such troughs or indeed peaks may be subject to a small error.

The other piece of information is that a line drawn through the centre of this average corresponds to a value of about 90 to 95, suggesting this is a constant amount which has been added to the cycles.

201-day average

Since we have discovered a wavelength of around 200, we can now apply a centred average of period 201. The result of doing this is shown in Figure 8.10. This is very informative since this has removed all the various cycles, leaving an almost straight line at a level of about 100. We can now say with confidence that if all the cycles have been removed, the resulting straight line represents the original line of value 100 points which was added into the mixture. We can also say that there are no cycles with wavelengths appreciably more than 201, since these would still be apparent in the output from the 201-point average.

Figure 8.10 – A centred average of period 201 days has been applied to the complex waveform. The result is an almost straight line at a value of 100 points.

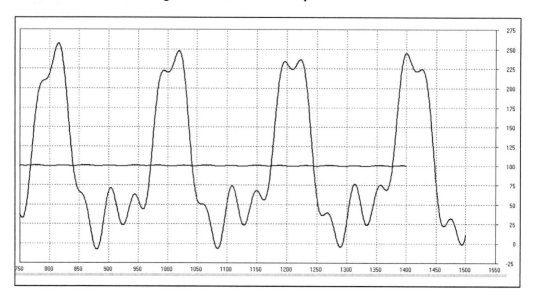

101-day average

We can now go through a sequence of testing a few averages with periods between 51 and 151. The simplest output is that given by a 101-day average. This is shown in Figure 8.11. This shows the cycle of period 201 days to be only slightly distorted.

Figure 8.11 – A centred average of period 101 days has been applied. The output is a good representation of the original 201-day cycle. The amplitude is about 60 points.

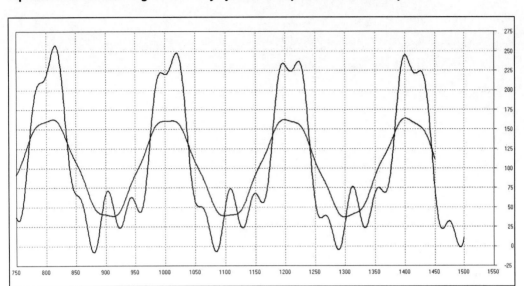

Since, of course, the application of a moving average will attenuate the cycle to an extent depending upon the relative values for wavelength and period of the average, it is to be expected that the amplitude of the 201-day cycle which has been isolated in this way will be reduced. This is true, since the amplitude of this cycle is only 62 units (half of the trough-to-peak height).

We have come as far as we can in the analysis of this complex set of three cycles, having found that there is a cycle of wavelength 201 days and amplitude greater than 62, plus a straight line with a value of 100 units.

We cannot isolate the cycles of wavelength 41 and 101 because if we use an average of period between 101 and 201 we will remove the cycles of wavelength 41 and 101 for the reasons stated earlier in the chapter. If we use an average of period between 41 and 101 we will remove the cycle of wavelength 41 but leave a mixture of the cycles of period 101 and 201. The amplitude of the cycle of wavelength 101 coming through in the output will depend upon how close the period of the average is to 101. The further towards 41 the period being used, the greater will be the amplitude of the cycle of wavelength 101 in the output. In other words, all we can hope to do is to isolate a mixture of cycles of wavelength 101 and 201.

Thus from our experiments with applying centred moving averages to mixtures of cycles we can see that the only cycle we can isolate from a mixture is the one with highest wavelength.

From this simple set of experiments we can reach a very important conclusion. For any value of period used for an average upon a mixture of cycles, the resulting output is essentially the sum of all cycles with wavelength greater than the period used for the average.

If there is a wide gap in wavelengths between the highest two wavelengths, as was the case with this example, then we can isolate the cycle with the highest wavelength when an average is used with period equal to the second highest wavelength. This removes this second highest cycle totally and greatly reduces the amplitude of those cycles of shorter wavelength.

This gives us an important understanding of what a centred moving average represents when applied to market data and is the key to predicting future trends by using moving averages.

Moving average differences

Although it would appear that by using the methods discussed so far we can only isolate the cycle with highest wavelength, there is another property of moving averages than we can use to our advantage. We have already shown that an average with the same period as the wavelength of a cycle to which it is applied removes that cycle. The question is, where does this 'lost' data go, and can we retrieve it? The fact is, it isn't lost, and can easily be retrieved.

It has gone to form the difference between the output of the moving average and the data itself. For each value of the centred average, the difference between that value and the value of the data itself at that point will re-form the lost cycle. This is demonstrated in Figure 8.12. We can see that the vertical lines (which represent the difference) outline the original cycle. It might be more accurate to say that the values of these differences when plotted would be the original cycle. Note also that the amplitude of the reconstituted cycle is identical to that of the original.

> **"** The only cycle we can isolate from a mixture is the one with highest wavelength. **"**

Figure 8.12 – The differences between the value of the centred average and the data itself will re-form the original cycle.

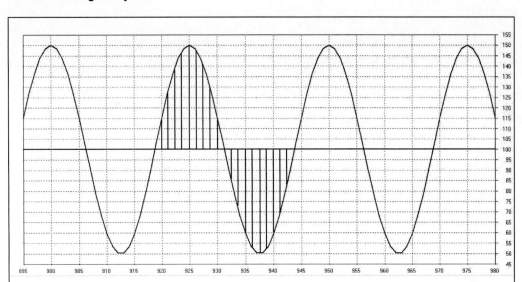

This is known as an average difference and will allow us to isolate the cycle of lowest wavelength from the complex mixture. Note that it is absolutely essential that a centred average is used, since the differences obtained from an average with no lag will be meaningless.

41-day average difference

If we apply a 41-point average difference to the mixture of cycles shown in Figure 8.8 we get the result shown in Figure 8.13. The cycle shown in the lower panel has a wavelength of 41 days if the peak-to-peak or trough-to-trough distances are measured.

Figure 8.13 – The 41-point average difference of the mixture of cycles shown in Figure 8.8.

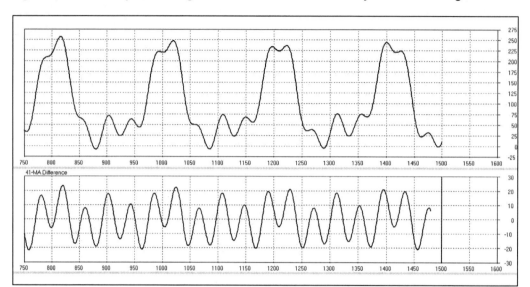

Although the isolated cycle is not absolutely clean, since there is a slight interference from the other cycles which causes the peaks and troughs not to lie in straight lines, there is no doubt at all that we have isolated and can identify the 41-day cycle. It is important also to note that the peaks and troughs of this cycle are in the same positions in time as the original 41-day cycle which was put into the mixture of cycles.

101-day average difference

In these two exercises we have isolated the 201-day cycle and the 41-day cycle. Neither of the methods that we have shown will isolate the 101-day cycle. To prove this point, the 101-point average difference is shown in Figure 8.14.

Figure 8.14 – The 101-point average difference of the mixture of cycles shown in Figure 8.8 does not isolate the 101-day cycle.

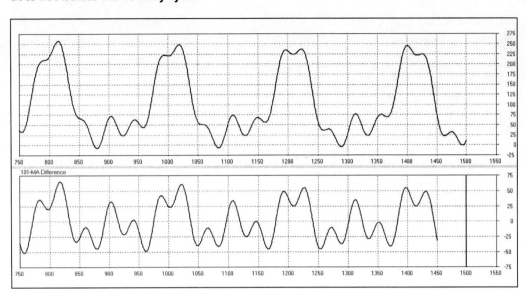

In this plot we still see in the lower panel a complex pattern which is due to the combination of the 41-day and 101-day cycles.

Comparison of centred averages with average differences

From the discussion so far, two very important points have been established from the properties of centred moving averages and average differences.

The **centred average** represents essentially the sum of all those cycles with wavelength greater than the period of the average. The greater the difference between the wavelength of a cycle and this period, the greater is the influence of this cycle on this sum.

The **centred average difference** represents essentially the sum of all those cycles with wavelength equal to or less than the period of the average. The less the difference between the wavelength of a cycle and this period, the greater the influence of this cycle is on this sum.

Thus we are still faced with the problem of how to isolate the 101-day cycle.

Difference of two averages

The average difference method just described is actually a special case of a more general method. This is to calculate the differences between two centred averages. Thus the average difference discussed earlier is the case where the second average has a period of one.

The two averages should be chosen so as to bracket the wavelength which it is desired to isolate. In the present case, periods of 135 and 51 were chosen, but a wide range of values can be used. The result of using these two values is shown in Figure 8.15.

Figure 8.15 – The difference between the 51-point and 135-point centred averages is shown as the filled in portions of the plot. The original cycle data has been omitted for clarity.

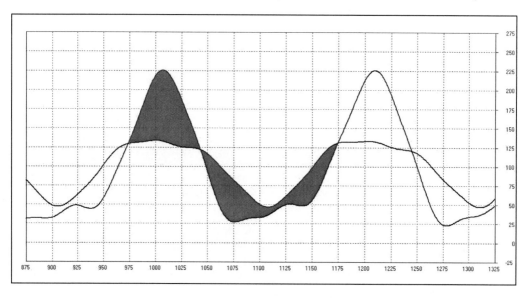

The original complex mixture of cycles has been omitted for clarity. The difference between the two averages is shown as filled in to highlight the process. When these differences are plotted, the cycle becomes obvious, as shown in the lower panel of Figure 8.16.

Figure 8.16 – The result of plotting the differences between the two averages is shown in the lower panel.

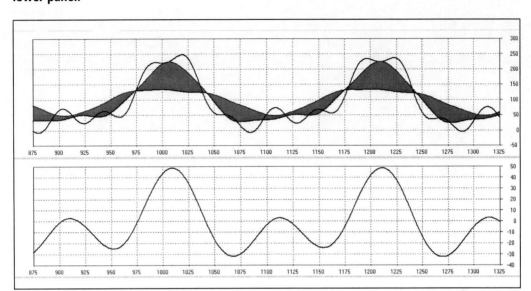

The two prominent peaks are separated by 202 days and since these represent two sweeps of the cycle, this is equivalent to a wavelength of 101 days. However, there is some distortion of the overall plot, so that the amplitude does not remain stable across the whole section. It is also worth pointing out that the difference between the positions of the prominent peaks and the next lesser peak is 104 days. In other words the minor peaks do not sit exactly halfway between the prominent peaks.

In spite of these two difficulties, we can see quite clearly that the use of the difference between two centred averages is an excellent way of isolating individual cycles from a complex mixture.

9

Averages as Proxies for Trends

In this chapter we will build upon the discussion in Chapters 7 and 8. We will do this by applying various centred moving averages to market data and seeing the effect of using different values for the period. When the moving average is plotted as a centred average, as in Figure 9.1, one feature will be obvious. That is the oscillation of the data around the average.

Figure 9.1 – A centred 15-day moving average applied to the Motorola stock price. The price oscillates around the average but remains within certain limits.

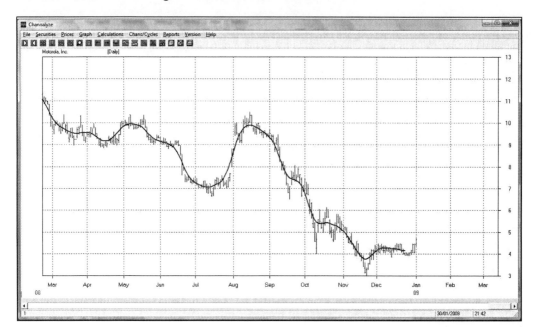

In the terms we used in Chapter 7 the centred average represents a trend. From our earlier definition (Chapter 7), whether this is a short-, medium- or long-term trend depends upon the period used for the average. Thus a short-term trend is caused by cycles of period 10 to 60 days, a medium-term trend by cycles of period 60 to 400 days and a long-term trend by cycles of period over 400 days.

15-day average

An average of period 15 days will remove cycles with wavelengths less than or equal to 15 days and remove to a lesser extent cycles which are longer in wavelength. The attenuation of these cycles decreases as their wavelengths increase. In this context therefore this average represents all of the trends – short, medium and long, except for very short-term trends which have wavelengths equal to or less than 15.

101-day average

In Figure 9.2 we show the same data with a centred 101-day moving average applied.

Figure 9.2 – A centred 101-day moving average applied to the Motorola stock price. The price oscillates around the average but remains within certain limits.

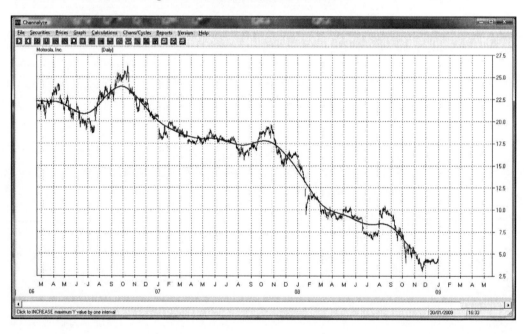

An average of period 101 days will remove cycles with wavelengths less than or equal to 101 days and remove to a lesser extent cycles which have a longer wavelength. The attenuation of these cycles decreases as their wavelengths increase. In the context of the definition of timescales, this average represents two of the trends – medium and long.

501-day average

Shown in Figure 9.3 is the result of applying a centred average of period 501 days. Since this is over 400 days, this average represents the long-term trend.

Figure 9.3 – A centred 501-day moving average applied to the Motorola stock price. The price oscillates around the average but remains within certain limits.

As we see in Figure 9.3, and which was discussed briefly in Chapter 8, if we take the centred average to represent the trend, then because it terminates half a span of the average back in time, we have no idea at first glance as to the current state of the trend. Is it still headed downwards or has it changed direction during this gap of half of its period? In the case of the 501-day average in Figure 9.3, this gap amounts to 250 days, which is about one year of business days. As we have seen during the past year, huge moves in the market can and do occur over such a long period.

Oscillation of data around an average

The feature common to these three averages is of course that the data oscillates around them. A closer inspection shows that there is a limit to these oscillations in the sense that the excursions of the price data from the centred average reach a certain maximum before reversing direction. These excursions increase in extent as we move from the short-term average via the medium-term average to the long-term average. It is these excursions that we can turn into values that will produce probabilities for us. Of course, since these are centred averages, each one will terminate half a span back in time from the latest data point.

Probabilities From Centred Averages

We saw in the last chapter that the differences between a centred average and the data at each point in time were called, quite logically, average differences. It is worth restating what centred averages and centred average differences represent.

1. The centred average represents essentially the sum of all those cycles with wavelength greater than the period of the average. The less the difference between the wavelength of a cycle and this period, the greater the influence of this cycle on this sum.

2. The centred average difference represents essentially the sum of all those cycles with wavelength equal to or less than the period of the average. The less the difference between the wavelength of a cycle and this period, the greater the influence of this cycle on this sum.

How data is distributed around the centred average

Imagine stretching out the average so that it becomes a straight line with the data still dispersed about it in the same way as the original. Now imagine looking down the whole length of this line. The effect is shown in Figure 9.4. The position of the average is shown by the vertical line in the centre of the rectangle. The -ve and +ve represent the extremes of movement below and above the position of the average. Quite clearly the data spends more time near the position of the average than it does at the extremes. It is from this distribution around the average that we can deduce the probabilities, just as was done for the daily changes in Chapter 4.

Figure 9.4 – How the data is distributed around the position of the average. The -ve and +ve extremes denote the furthest that the data moves from the position of the average.

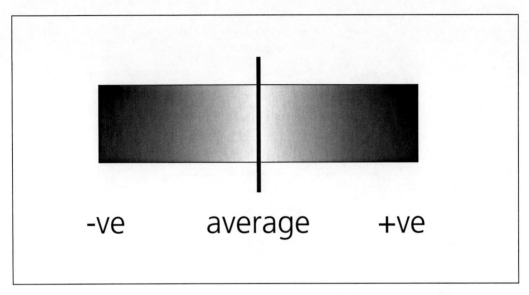

-ve   average   +ve

Obviously since the data spends very little time at the extremes, these represent **low probability positions**, whereas **the centre portion represents a high probability area**. Quite clearly, if the data is in a low probability area, it is unlikely to stay there as more data points arrive and the probability is high (but not 100%!) that it will move back towards the centre.

Numerical data

Distribution around the 15-day average

Figure 9.4 indicates that the price spends most of the time in the middle third of the whole range of differences. This is confirmed by Figure 9.5. This shows the distribution of Motorola closing prices about the 15-day centred average which was shown in Figure 9.1.

Figure 9.5 – The distribution of Motorola data around the centred 15-day moving average. The data has been sorted into 200 bins (slots) and the vertical axis is the number of values that fall into each bin.

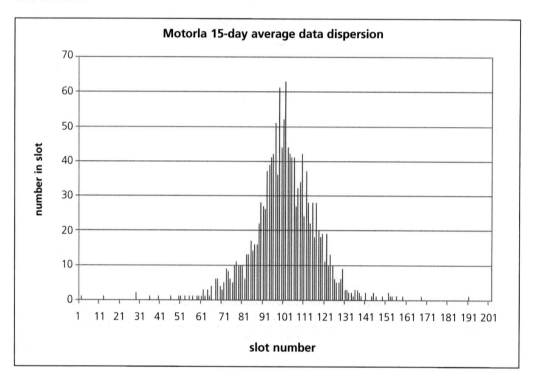

The data was allocated into one or other of 201 bins. The centre bin, bin number 101, corresponds to the position of the moving average itself. Bin 1 corresponds to the largest negative value, i.e. when the price is below the average line and at an extreme value. Bin 201 corresponds to the largest positive value, i.e. when the price is above the average and at an extreme value.

This type of distribution is of course familiar from Chapter 4, in which the distribution of daily price changes was investigated. Quite clearly, the price data spends most of its time around the centre position of the moving average (bin 101) and very little time at the extremes. Since these data are a set of numerical values, we can, just as in Chapter 4, use the concept of standard deviation to determine probabilities if we make the assumption that these data are normally distributed.

As was stated in Chapter 4, in a normal distribution:

- 68.27% of the points lie within one standard deviation of the mean

- 95.45% of the points lie within two standard deviations of the mean

- 99.73% of the points lie within two standard deviations of the mean.

If the data are normally distributed then we can produce probabilities for the location of any future particular data point relative to a known position of the centred moving average. However, as we saw previously, calculating exact probabilities is not a straightforward process and approximate values will serve us well enough for the purposes of this chapter. All we need in our approach is to grasp the fact that there is a low probability that a data point should be at the extreme left or extreme right of the plot shown in Figure 9.5. If, therefore, a data point is already in this position, then it is highly unlikely to stay there, and the next values should move towards the area of high probability, i.e. the central position of the average.

The standard deviation of the values displayed in Figure 9.5 was $13.3859. Two standard deviations amount to a value of $27 (rounded off). Therefore we can say that 95% of the points lie between bins 74 and 128.

Distribution around 101-day average

In Figure 9.6 we show the dispersion of Motorola data around the 101-day centred average. The distribution in this case is much flatter than was the case for the 15-day average. The standard deviation in this case was $7.76. Therefore, in round numbers, two standard deviations are $15. Thus we can say that 95% of the points lie between bins 86 and 116.

Quite clearly therefore the spread of bins that contains 95% of the values is much higher in the case of the 15-day average than it is in the case of the 101-day average.

Figure 9.6 – The dispersion of Motorola data around the centred 101-day moving average. The data has been sorted into 200 bins (slots) and the vertical axis is the number of values that fall into each bin.

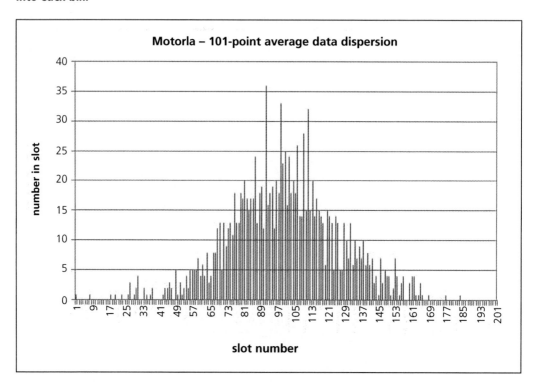

In Figure 9.7 we show the dispersion of Motorola data around the 501-day centred average. The distribution in this case is much flatter than was the case for the 15-day average. The standard deviation in this case was $4.8. In round numbers therefore, two standard deviations are $10. Thus we can say that 95% of the points lie between bins 91 and 111.

Figure 9.7 – The dispersion of Motorola data around the centred 501-day moving average. The data has been sorted into 200 bins (slots) and the vertical axis is the number of values that fall into each bin.

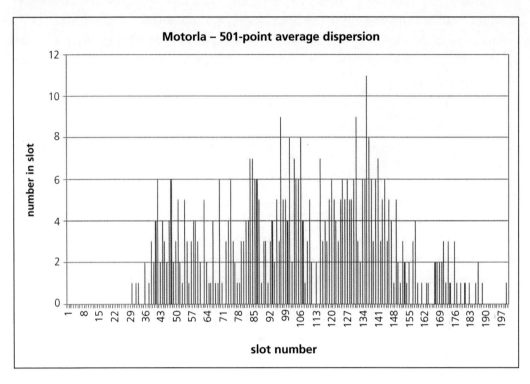

Quite clearly therefore the spread of bins that contains 95% of the values is much higher in the case of the 15-day average and 101-day average than it is in the case of the 501-day average.

This gradual erosion of the usefulness of using probability and distribution around moving averages echoes that discussed at the end of Chapter 4 for longer-term price changes. The practical limit for the period of the average in carrying out such studies is around 201.

Boundaries and Channels

The advantage of putting the differences between the centred average and the associated data point into bins is that it is easy to calculate which two bin numbers will frame, say, 95% of the values between them. As shown above, the calculation of standard deviation will enable these two bins to be defined. As we saw, for the 15-point average they were 75 and 127, for the 101-point average they were 86 and 116, and for the 501-point average they were 91 and 111.

Knowing the bin numbers, we can see what value of distance from the central average these represent and then draw lines at this constant value below and above the centred average line. This approach is shown for the 101-point centred average in Figure 9.8. Here we have drawn constant depth lines above and below the centred average. This can also be done with a pencil on a chart on which is plotted a centred 101-day average. From the bin numbers it is simple to calculate the positions of these lines so that, for example, only 5% of the data points lie outside these boundaries. These boundaries then constitute a channel, which is why this method is called channel analysis. Using such a visual method rather than staying with numerical distributions makes it very much easier to understand what is happening to the data as it oscillates around the central average line.

Quite clearly, as shown in Figure 9.8, there is a high probability that the price will retreat once it reaches the boundary. Since in this particular case the boundaries are set so that only 5% of the data points will lie outside, there are some points of approach to the boundary in which the boundary is then penetrated. However, this is only temporary, since there is a low probability of the next data point to arrive remaining in this location.

Figure 9.8 – The centred 101-point average now has a line at a constant distance above and below the average. The position of these lines has been chosen such that only 5% of the data points lie outside of them.

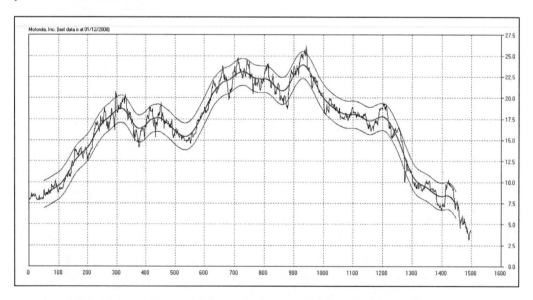

These points of penetration are shown in better detail in Figure 9.9.

Figure 9.9 – This expanded portion of Figure 9.8 shows the points of penetration of the boundaries.

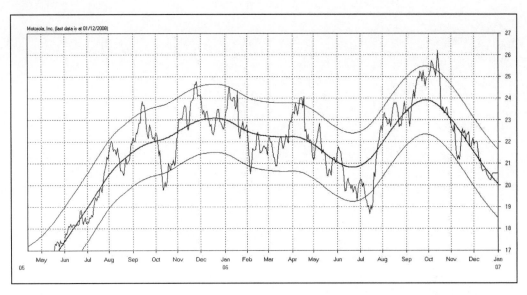

It is possible with the Channalyze software to adjust the position of the boundary so as to increase or decrease the number of data points which lie outside the boundary. In Figure 9.10 the channel boundaries have been adjusted so that no points lie outside the channel. However, this may be counter-productive. In Figure 9.10 the price movement did not reach a boundary from May 2003 until July 2006. Since the idea behind channel analysis is to provide buying and selling signals, this situation of zero points lying outside of the channel would have been ineffective over that period of time. As always in trading there is a balance to be struck between too many signals which might be false and too few so that traders will remain inactive for too long.

Figure 9.10 – Here the channel boundaries have been adjusted so that no points lie outside the channel.

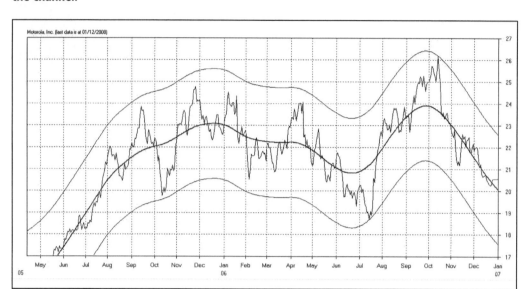

What channels tell us

We saw from Chapter 8 that the centred average represents essentially the sums of all of those cycles of wavelength greater than the period used for the average.

The movement of the price data within the channel is due of course to the sum of all of those cycles which have wavelengths less than or equal to the period used for the centred average upon which the channel is based. Using a channel to analyse the price movement separates the trends into two categories, thus enabling a better focus on the overall movement of the stock:

1. The channel itself represents the longer-term trend – whether this is short-, medium- or long-term depends on the value chosen for the average.

2. The movement within the channel represents the shorter-term trend – whether this is short-, medium- or long-term depends on the value chosen for the average.

This point about the movement of price data within the channel representing the sum of cycles with wavelengths less than the period of the average can be demonstrated in another way. This is done by plotting the 101-point average difference. This plot is shown in Figure 9.11.

Figure 9.11 – The upper panel shows the 101-day channel and the lower panel the 101-day average difference.

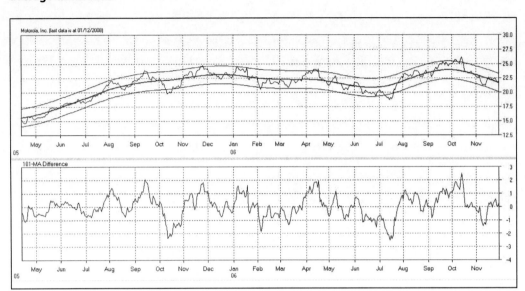

The correspondence between the movement within the channel in the upper panel and the movement in the average difference is quite clear. Points where the data reaches the channel boundaries are replicated by peaks and troughs in the lower trace.

Prediction of future price

What we have discussed so far enables us to predict a range in which the price will move relative to the centred average. Thus we are still faced with the fact that we do not know how the average has behaved over the half of its period which covers the period of time from the last calculated point to the present time and then on into the future. Unless we can make a good prediction of the path which the average (which represents the trend) has taken over this period of time, then any prediction of the price relative to this central trend will be of little value.

Extrapolating the centred average

The dilemma facing us is exemplified by Figure 9.12. In this we show just three ways out of the many in which a particular centred average can be extrapolated into the future. This has been done by taking into account the curvature of the most recent section of the centred average and projecting it into the future. How large a section which is taken can have a profound effect on the extrapolation. Thus in the absence of any other evidence there is a large error associated with any method which simply depends on a visual estimate. However, there are several ways in which we can make progress. The first is through probability analysis, the second through channel analysis and the third is through cycle analysis. The most powerful technique for predicting future trends and price movement around these trends will be that in which all three of these are used. This approach is discussed in more detail in the final chapter of this book.

Figure 9.12 – There are many ways of extrapolating a centred average from its last calculated point to the present and into the future. Each of the three possibilities shown above can be justified.

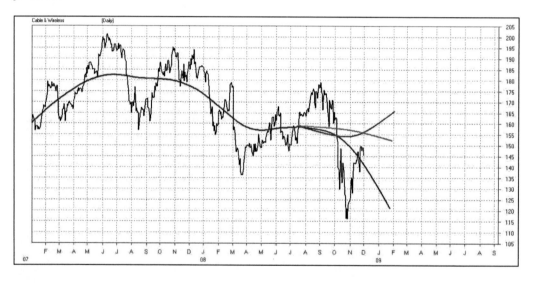

Where channel analysis will be able to help us is in establishing a probable location for the boundaries. Since the average is in the exact middle of the channel, it follows that knowing the position of the boundaries will give us the position of the average and hence of the trend which it represents. We will be able to do this because of the fact that boundaries are places where the price movement has a high probability of reversing direction. Therefore, of necessity, these reversals take the form of a peak or trough. It is by a careful examination of the position of these peaks and troughs that we can estimate the position of the boundaries. This method of establishing trend direction is discussed in Chapters 11 and 12.

10

Trend Turning Points (I)

In the last chapter we illustrated the dilemma that we face when we use centred averages as proxies for trends. We have a gap of half of the period of the average during which we do not know what the average (trend) has been doing. Before we can begin to think about the future movement of the trend we have to examine ways in which we can make a decent estimate of its current position.

Figure 9.12 from the last chapter is presented again here as Figure 10.1 in order to focus on what is required. The average is known up to the point where it divides into three possible paths.

Figure 10.1 – This centred average could be extrapolated in many ways to bring it up to the present time and into the future. The three paths shown are just three examples, each of which can be justified.

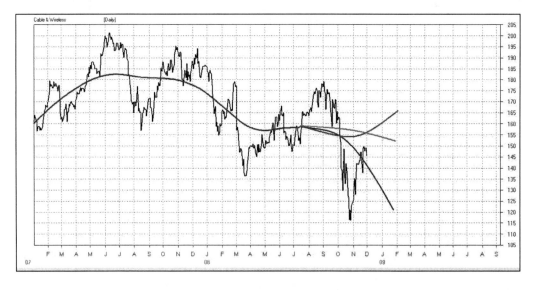

These three are used for illustrative purposes – there will be a large number of possible paths, each of which can be justified by analysis of the price data itself; so how do we bring these possibilities down to just one? The answer of course is that we cannot end up with just one line which represents the path of the average up to the present time. It might be possible in some circumstances to be able to draw the most probable path as a widening range of values as we move forwards from the last calculated point. This is shown in Figure 10.2, where there are limits to its probable position. By this it is meant that there is a range of values (the lowest value and highest value) within which there is a certain probability (say 90%) that the price will lie.

Figure 10.2 – It might be possible to extrapolate the average and put 90% limits on its probable position.

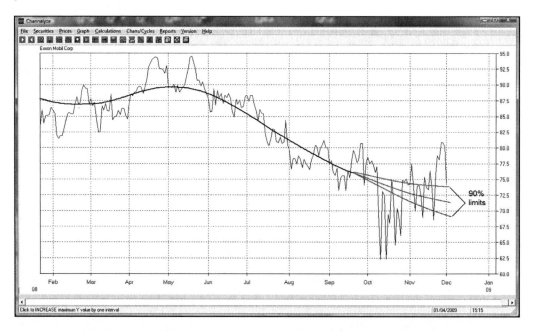

If it is not possible to predict a probable path for the extrapolated average, then the least we would hope to achieve is to decide whether it has changed direction somewhere within the gap. In this case it is not necessary to decide at which exact point it changed direction, but only that it has changed direction.

Short-term Trends

The simplest measure of determining whether a trend (average) is currently standing at a higher or lower value than its last true calculated point is to obtain a prediction of its probable value at a future point.

This issue can be addressed by reference to the drop point, which was discussed in Chapter 8. A falling average will change direction if the new point being brought into the calculation is of greater value than the point being dropped. For a rising average, it will change direction if the new point being brought into the calculation is of lesser value than the point being dropped.

How can we estimate if a new point is likely to be of greater or less value than the point being dropped? The answer lies in the probability distribution of daily changes. We need to know:

1. the value of the drop point

2. the probability that the value of the new point lies above or below a certain value, this value being that required to offset the value being lost by the drop point.

Using these values we can extend the centred average incrementally from its last calculated point half a span back in time, one point at a time to the present.

Turning point in rising averages

Taking a nine-point centred average as an example, the initial position is shown in Figure 10.3. For ease of understanding, the x-axis has been labelled with point numbers rather than dates. The vertical line at point 1353 is the point at which the data terminates with a value of $49.95. The smoother line is the nine-point centred average. This terminates at point 1349, which is half a span (four points) back.

Figure 10.3 – The centred nine-point moving average calculated with the last data point being at point 1353 (12 May 2008). The data to the right of the vertical line shows the subsequent price movement.

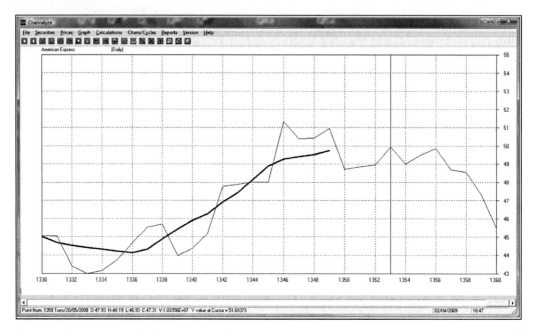

The issue now is to move this average on, one point at a time, to the present. In reality, as each new data point comes in, the average needs to be recalculated so that its position will move on one point at a time. Thus, once we know the value of point 1354, we can calculate the value of the average for point 1350. Once we know the value of point 1355, we can calculate the value of the average at point 1351, and so on. The value of the average at the present time, i.e. point 1351, will only be known once we have the value of the data at point 1355, which is four days into the future. In general, therefore, to bring an n-point average up to the present time, we need to estimate the value of the data points up to half a span (n is odd, so half a span is (1 - n)/2) into the future. In the case of this nine-point average, this means that we have to estimate the next four points into the future. The only way we can do this is to use the probabilities associated with the distribution of price changes as discussed in Chapter 4. Thus we will need the distribution of one-day, two-day, three-day and four-day changes and determine the appropriate probabilities for these various price changes.

Since in Figure 10.3 the average is rising, our interest is in seeing when or if it has changed direction between point 1349 and 1353. This is where the drop point becomes essential. When we compute a new value for the average, we will bring in the estimated value at point 1354, but will drop the point 10 days back, i.e. point 1345. Thus, in order for the average to start falling, the new value must be less than that at point 1345, i.e. less than $48.42. Since the value at point 1353 is $49.95, then this can only be achieved if the one-day change from point 1353 to 1354 is a fall of more than $1.53.

The distribution of two-day changes in American Express is shown in Figure 10.4. The probability of a fall of more than $1.53 is only 4.4%. Thus it is highly improbable that the average is falling at point 1350.

Figure 10.4 – The distribution of the American Express two-day price changes. The probability of a change of less than $1.38 can be seen to be 91.5%. Therefore the probability of a rise equal to or greater than this is 8.5%.

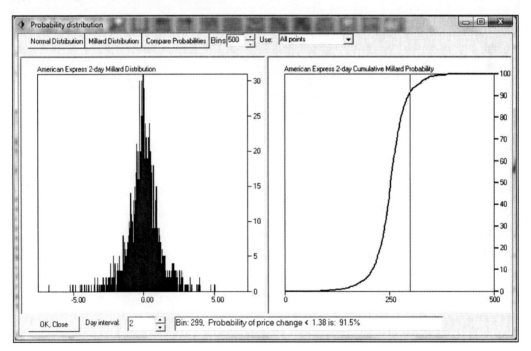

The next step would be to determine the distribution of two-day changes in order to estimate whether point 1355 will fall enough to cause the average also to fall. Then, a three-day distribution will give us this information for point 1356 and finally a four-day distribution will give us the information for point 1357, which will bring the average up to date.

The data obtained by this process is shown in Table 10.1.

The probabilities in Table 10.1 would lead one to believe that the average is likely to change direction by the time the estimated data for point 1357 is determined.

Table 10.1 – The probability of the price changes being sufficient to keep the nine-point centred average rising.

Average point	Average value	Drop point	Drop value	New data point	Value	Value required	Must be >	Probability %
1347	49.43	1342	47.77	1351	48.85			
1348	49.53	1343	47.89	1352	48.96			
1349	49.74	1344	48.01	1353	49.95			
1350	-	1345	48.02	1354	-	48.02	-1.93	97.5
1351	-	1346	51.33	1355	-	51.33	1.38	8.5
1352	-	1347	50.4	1356	-	50.4	0.45	31.7

The probabilities in the last column of Table 10.1 were obtained from the one-, two- and three-day distributions as discussed in Chapter 4. The two-day distribution is shown in Figure 10.4. This shows that the probability of the price change being greater than $1.38 is only 8.5%. Thus the probability of it being less than $1.38 is 100 - 8.5 = 91.5%.

From Table 10.1 it can be seen that the probability of the average still rising at point 1350 is over 97%, so that we do not expect it to change direction at that point. However, the probability of it still rising at point 1351 is now only 8.5%, so that we have a high expectation that the average will have turned down at that point. This means that the maximum point should occur at point 1350 on the previous day. In Figure 10.5 we show how the average actually moved when its values were calculated from data which terminated much later on.

Figure 10.5 – The actual path of the centred nine-day average in American Express. The average topped out at point 1350, 7 May 2008.

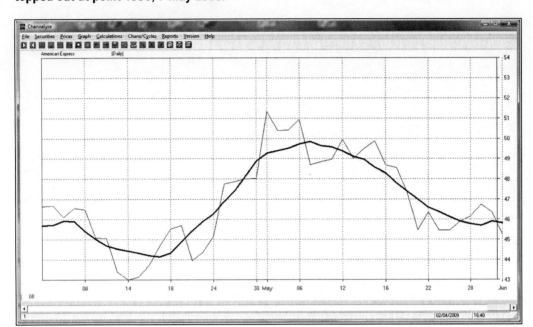

It can be seen that the average did indeed top out at point 1350 on 7 May 2008.

Thus it appears that we have a useful method of determining the probability that an average has changed direction. However, as discussed in Chapter 4, there will be a limit for the spans (periods) of the averages to which this method might be applied. For averages with longer periods, the Millard version of the Monte Carlo simulation should be employed (see Chapter 11).

Turning point in falling averages

We can now test this method on a longer period of average – 15 days – and also on a situation where we are trying to predict whether the average will change direction and start to rise. In Figure 10.6 we show a plot of the AT&T stock price with a 15-day centred average superimposed.

Figure 10.6 – The centred 15-point average calculated with the last data point 1307, 7 March 2008.

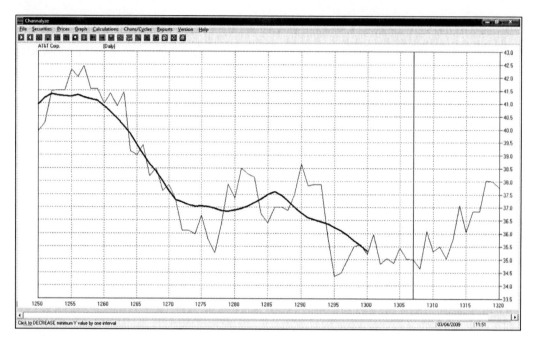

Since in Figure 10.6 the average is falling, our interest is in seeing when or if it has changed direction between point 1292 and 1307. When we compute a new value for the average, we will bring in the estimated value at point 1307, but will drop the point 15 days back, i.e. point 1292. Thus, in order for the average to start rising, the new value must be greater than that at point 1292, i.e. more than $37.88. Since the value at point 1307 is $35.01, then this can only be achieved if the one-day change from point 1307 to 1308 is a rise of more than $2.87.

We can follow the same procedure for this example as we did for the previous one. The various data points and probabilities are listed in Table 10.2.

From Table 10.2 it can be seen that the probability of the average still falling at point 1301 is over 99%, so that we do not expect it to change direction at that point. The same applies to point 1302, in which the probability of it still falling is over 94%. However, when we come to point 1303, the probability of it still falling is now only 13.25%, so that we have a high expectation that the average will have turned up at that point. This means that the minimum point should occur at point 1302.

Table 10.2 – The probability of the price changes being sufficient to keep the 15-point centred average falling.

Average point	Average value	Drop point	Drop value	New data point	Value	Value required	Must be <	Probability %
1299	49.53	-						
1300	49.74	1292	37.88	1307	35.01			
1301	-	1293	37.88	1308	-	37.88	2.87	99.66
1302	-	1294	35.89	1309	-	35.89	0.89	94.71
1303	-	1295	34.36	1310	-	34.36	-0.65	13.25
1304		1296	34.47	1311	-	34.47	-0.54	21.7

The distribution of three-day changes for AT&T is shown in Figure 10.7. It can be seen that the probability of a change of less than -0.7 is 13.25%. This value is used in Table 10.2 because it is the closest to the required value of -0.65.

Figure 10.7 – The distribution of the AT&T three-day price changes. The probability of a change of less than $0.7 can be seen to be 13.25%. Therefore the probability of a rise in the average is 86.75%.

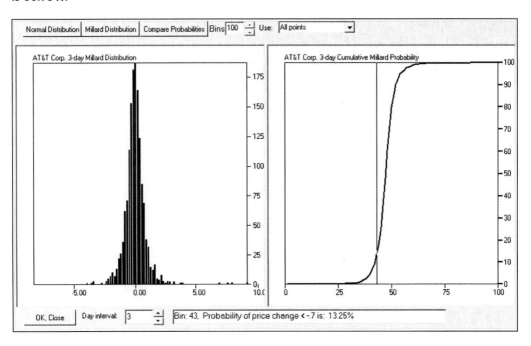

In Figure 10.8 we show how the average actually moved when its values were calculated from data which terminated much later on. The minimum occurred at point 1301 on 28 February 2008. We were only one day out in predicting the turning point of this average!

Figure 10.8 – The actual movement of the 15-point centred average over the period for which the prediction was being made.

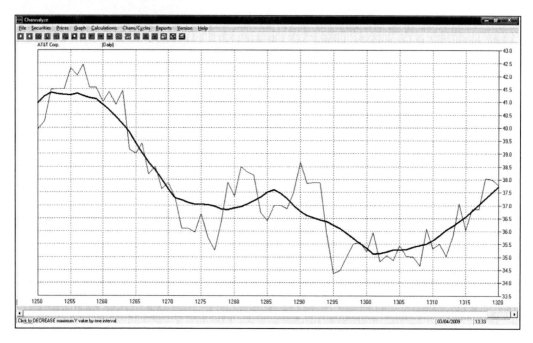

Rising average continuing to rise

As well as being able to determine that an average may have changed direction in the gap between the last calculated point and the present time, it is also useful to be able to determine that an average will not change direction.

Shown in Figure 10.9 is a section of the American Express stock price with the nine-point centred average superimposed. The average has been rising for some time, so the issue is whether it is still rising at the point corresponding to the last data point.

Figure 10.9 – A rising nine-point centred average in the American Express stock price. The issue is whether it is still rising at the current time. This point is at the position of the vertical line.

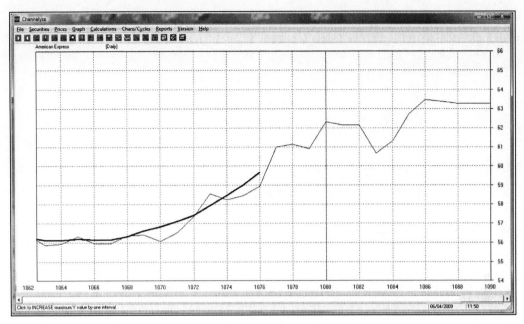

Using the same procedure as was shown in Table 10.1 for a rising nine-point centred average in American Express, the data shown in Table 10.3 were obtained.

Table 10.3 – The probability of the price changes being sufficient to keep the nine-point centred average rising.

Average point	Average value	Drop point	Drop value	New data point	Value	Value required	Must be >	Probability %
1074	58.51	1069	56.41	1078	61.15			
1075	59	1070	56.05	1079	60.91			
1076	59.67	1071	56.51	1080	60.52			
1077	-	1072	57.36	1081	-	57.36	-3.16	99.34
1078	-	1073	58.56	1082	-	58.56	-1.96	95.06
1079	-	1074	58.24	1083	-	58.24	-2.28	94.65

The last column shows that the probability is extremely high that the average will keep on rising. That it did indeed rise is shown in Figure 10.10.

Figure 10.10 – The nine-point centred average in the American Express stock price continues to rise as predicted by the probability calculations shown in Table 10.3.

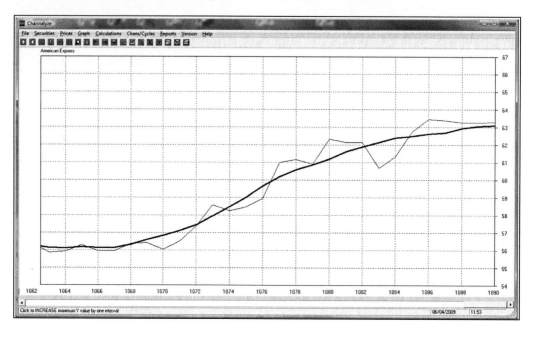

Falling average continuing to fall

Just as it was possible to determine that the average was still rising, then so we should be able to determine the probability that a falling average is still falling. This time we can use the example of the Eastman Kodak stock price with a 15-point average superimposed. This is calculated at 2 June 2008 and is shown in Figure 10.11.

Figure 10.11 – A falling 15-point centred average in the Eastman Kodak stock price as calculated on 2 June 2008. The issue is whether it is still falling at the current time. This point is at the position of the vertical line.

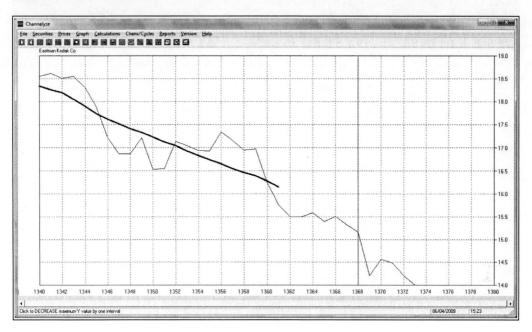

The calculation in Table 10.4 brings us right up to the last data point at 1376 and it can be seen that the high percentage probabilities would suggest that the centred average is still falling, although the probabilities are decreasing slowly. This is seen to be the case from the plot of this average calculated further on in time in Figure 10.12. The average did not stop falling for another eight days, finally bottoming out on 12 June 2008.

Table 10.4 – The probability of the price changes being sufficient to keep the 15-point centred average falling. Point 1368 on 2 June 2008 is the last real data point.

Average point	Average value	Drop point	Drop value	New data point	Value	Value required	Must be <	Probability %
1359	16.4	1351	16.55					
1360	16.28	1352	17.14	1367	15.32			
1361	16.16	1353	17.05	1368	15.16	-		
1362	-	1354	16.94	1369	-	16.94	1.78	99.46
1363	-	1355	16.93	1370	-	16.93	1.77	98.66
1364		1356	17.34	1371	-	17.34	2.18	96.65
1365		1357	17.15	1372	-	17.15	1.99	97.65
1366		1358	16.95	1373	-	16.95	1.79	96.24
1367		1359	16.98	1374	-	16.98	1.82	95.5
1368		1360	16.24	1375	-	16.24	1.08	86.44
1369		1361	15.76	1376	-	15.76	0.6	73.67

Figure 10.12 – The 15-point centred average in the Eastman Kodak stock price continues to fall as predicted by Table 10.4.

Quite clearly, we have a very powerful method for determining how a centred average, and thus the trend which it represents, has behaved from the last calculated point up to the present time. Without this knowledge many traders will take a position assuming a trend is rising or falling when in fact it has already changed direction. This change of direction will not become obvious until a few days into the future, when more data has arrived to update the position of the centred average.

Predicting turning points in the near future

The examples discussed so far have been those in which we investigated whether the average had changed direction in the gap between the last true value of the average and the latest data point. It was seen quite clearly that this method gave an excellent indication of changes of direction which occurred and also indicated where a change of direction did not occur.

It will have been noted that as far as the known drop points are concerned, we only needed to use enough to cover half a span of the average, which would bring us up to the present time. Since there are n drop points, where n is the span of the average, then we have enough extra drop points to be able to predict the path of the average up to half a span into the future. The question is, therefore, are we going to be as successful in these predictions?

In Table 10.5 we see the calculation of the probabilities of the average continuing to fall. There is no suggestion from these figures that the average will change direction. However, it was determined later from new data arriving that the average bottomed out at point 1376.

Table 10.5 – The probabilities of the 15-point centred average of Eastman Kodak stock continuing to fall out over the period of half a span into the future from the last data point at point 1372 on 6 June.

Average point	Average value	Drop point	Drop value	New data point	Value	Value required	Must be <	Probability %
1364	15.64	1356	17.34	1371	14.48	17.34		
1365	15.43	1357	17.15	1372	14.21	17.15		
1366		1358	16.95	1373	-	16.95	2.74	99.9
1367		1359	16.98	1374	-	16.98	2.77	99.9
1368		1360	16.24	1375	-	16.24	2.03	98.6
1369		1361	15.76	1376	-	15.76	1.55	95.6
1370		1362	15.5	1377	-	15.5	1.29	91.4
1371		1363	15.5	1378	-	15.5	1.29	90.3
1372		1364	15.59	1379	-	15.59	1.43	90
1373		1365	15.39	1380	-	15.39	1.18	84.9
1374		1366	15.51	1381	-	15.51	1.3	85.4
1375		1367	15.32	1382	-	15.32	1.11	81.9
1376		1368	15.16	1383	-	15.16	0.95	76.3
1377	turned	1369	14.21	1384	-	14.21	0	51.9
1378		1370	14.56	1385	-	14.56	0.35	59.9
1379		1371	14.48	1386	-	14.48	0.27	58.5

In order to check that this was not just a problem with particular values of the last data point and the drop points, the exercise was repeated from the next data point at 1373 (see Table 10.6), with a value of $13.57. Even without calculating the probabilities, it can be seen that the values labelled 'Must be<' are such that the probabilities will be high that the values will be less than these. As can be seen from the final column, there is no indication that the average changed direction on or about point 1377.

Table 10.6 – The probabilities of the 15-point centred average of Eastman Kodak stock continuing to fall out over the period of half a span into the future from the last data point at point 1373 on 9 June.

Average point	Average value	Drop point	Drop value	New data point	Value	Value required	Must be <	Probability %
1365	15.43	1357	17.15	1372	14.21	17.15		
1366	15.2	1358	16.95	1373	13.57	16.95		
1367		1359	16.98	1374	-	16.98	3.41	99.9
1368		1360	16.24	1375	-	16.24	2.67	99.7
1369		1361	15.76	1376	-	15.76	2.19	99
1370		1362	15.5	1377	-	15.5	1.93	97.8
1371		1363	15.5	1378	-	15.5	1.93	97.3
1372		1364	15.59	1379	-	15.59	2.02	95.7
1373		1365	15.39	1380	-	15.39	1.82	96
1374		1366	15.51	1381	-	15.51	1.94	93.3
1375		1367	15.32	1382	-	15.32	1.75	89.6
1376		1368	15.16	1383	-	15.16	1.59	69.4
1377		1369	14.21	1384	-	14.21	0.64	77.1
1378		1370	14.56	1385	-	14.56	1.89	73.9
1379		1371	14.48	1386	-	14.48	0.91	67.2
1380		1372	14.21	1387	-	14.21	0.64	68.2

Finally, in Table 10.7 we see the data estimated where we have made the last data point to be that at 1384, 13 June. It was not until we reached point 1388 that the probability fell below 50% that the average was still continuing downwards, i.e. a reasonable probability that the average had now bottomed out.

Table 10.7 – The probabilities of the 15-point centred average of Eastman Kodak stock continuing to fall out over the period of half a span into the future from the last data point at point 1377 on 13 June.

Average point	Average value	Drop point	Drop value	New data point	Value	Value required	Must be <	Probability %
1375	13.56	1367	15.32	1382	12.41	15.32	1.75	
1376	12.96	1368	15.16	1383	12.34	15.16	1.59	
1377		1369	14.21	1384	14.03	14.21	0.64	
1378		1370	14.56	1385		14.56	0.53	91.6
1379		1371	14.48	1386		14.48	0.45	79.9
1380		1372	14.21	1387		14.21	0.18	64.2
1381		1373	13.57	1388		13.57	-0.46	32.3
1382		1374	13.43	1389		13.43	-0.6	26.5
1383		1375	12.63	1390		12.63	-1.4	9.8
1384		1376	12.97	1391		12.97	-1.06	18.9

The exact path of the average over this period of time is shown in Figure 10.13. It can now be seen that the reason for the change in direction of the average was the large increase in price between point 1383, value $12.34, and point 1385, value $15.12 – a change of $2.78 over two days. The probability of this happening is less than 1% and hence it would not be predicted on the grounds of probability.

Figure 10.13 – The turning point in the 15-point centred average in the Eastman Kodak stock price was driven by the large rise in the stock price ($2.78) between points 1383 (23 June) and 1385 (25 June). The estimated probability of such a strong rise is less than 1%.

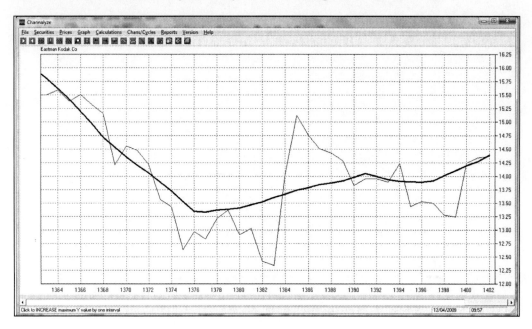

In conclusion, we have shown that the use of probability estimation is a very valuable tool in deciding whether an average has changed direction somewhere between the last calculated average point half a span in the past and the latest data point. It is not very useful in investigating if the average will change direction in the very near future, i.e. up to half a span into the future from the last data point.

11

Trend Turning Points (II)

In this chapter we will be examining more closely the properties of channel boundaries. The channel boundaries are of course constructed by drawing replicates of the centred average above and below the position of the average, and equidistant from it. Thus the channel is of constant depth throughout. This can be done by a computer program or by eye with a pencil and paper on the chart. The depth of the channel depends solely upon the level required for the probability that a new data point will lie within the channel. A good general value for this is 97.5%.

It is interesting that while the centred average is used to produce the boundaries, we can then use the boundaries which have been extrapolated to estimate the path the average might have taken across the gap. It can be seen that a few iterations of this process might be needed before a good estimate of the average can be obtained. This estimate will be particularly valuable when it comes to deciding whether the average, and hence the channel, has changed direction in this gap, or even if it might change direction in the very near future.

Estimation of Channel Direction

Shown in Figure 11.1 is the 101-point channel of the Brunswick Corporation stock price. A value of 96.5% has been chosen for the number of points allowed to be outside the channel. The vertical lines show the gap between the last true calculated point and the latest data point. The subsequent movement of the stock price is shown so that we can discuss how the analysis can proceed.

As the channel approaches the position of the last true point, it can be seen that in this case it is almost a straight line. This makes it easy to extrapolate, since the general rule in the first pass of extrapolation of channels is to maintain the previous rate of curvature. However, it is obvious that the extrapolation is not correct, since the stock price violates the upper boundary almost immediately at the position of the latest price. Since only 3.5% of points lie outside of the boundaries, then the upper boundary (and hence the lower boundary to preserve constant depth) will have to be raised at this point in order to preserve this allowable penetration.

Figure 11.1 – The 101-point channel of the Brunswick Corporation. The left-hand vertical line is the position of the last true calculated point of the average from which the channel is derived. The right-hand vertical line is the latest data point (4 September 2006). The subsequent movement of the stock price (not used in the calculation) is shown in order to clarify the discussion.

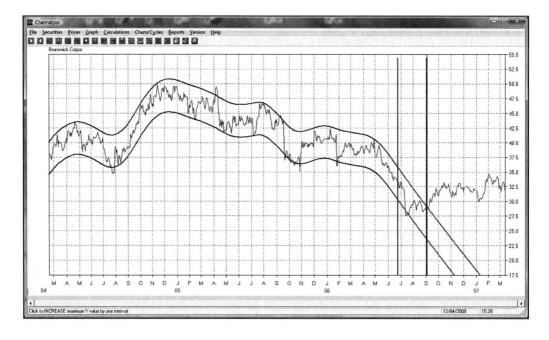

Of course, the boundary cannot simply be raised and its appearance as a straight line maintained at the same time. If this was attempted, then the trough which is shown within the gap would then violate the allowable level of penetration of the lower boundary. The only solution is to begin to bend the channel so that its rate of fall will begin to lessen.

The general approach therefore is to check boundaries for penetration by the stock price and make the appropriate adjustment while checking that this does not cause a penetration of the opposite boundary. This will inevitably mean that the rate of curvature will be changed. The position of the extrapolated boundary when new data are available for 12 September for the Brunswick Corporation is shown in Figure 11.2. This simply takes the curve of the actual channel and extrapolates it to the current last data point. Note that the additional data points have now introduced a slight bend into the channel even before any further adjustment is carried out.

Figure 11.2 – By 12 September the new data has caused the channel to curve slightly. The channel has not yet been adjusted to account for the data point at the latest position being above the upper boundary.

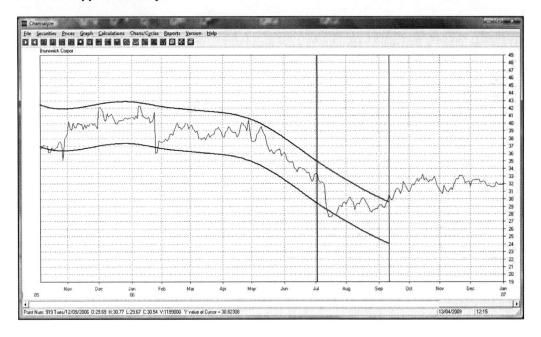

Shown in Figure 11.3 is the effect of a minor adjustment in the curvature of the extrapolated portion of the channel. The curvature has now increased and the channel appears to be about to bottom out.

Figure 11.3 – The channel has now been adjusted to account for the data point ($30.54) at the latest position (12 September) being above the upper boundary. Note the curvature has now increased and there is now the possibility that the channel is about to bottom out.

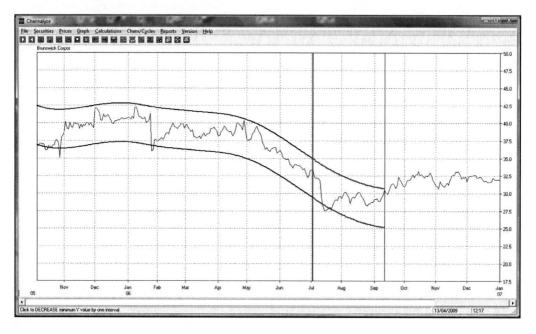

A few days later (20 September) the bend in the channel had to be increased by an adjustment in order to accommodate the fact that the new data point ($31.4) was again above the upper boundary. The result of adjusting the boundaries is shown in Figure 11.4. Quite clearly, therefore, the adjustment which was needed to preserve the low percentage of points allowed outside of the boundaries has shown that the channel has bottomed out and is now on its way upwards. The estimated low point of the channel from this analysis is at point 912 on 1 September.

This estimated low point is about halfway across the gap between the last calculated point and the last data point. It is interesting to check with later data how accurate this estimation was.

Figure 11.4 – The channel has now been adjusted to account for the data point ($31.4) at the latest position (20 September) being above the upper boundary. Note the increasing curvature now shows that the channel has bottomed out and is expected to rise.

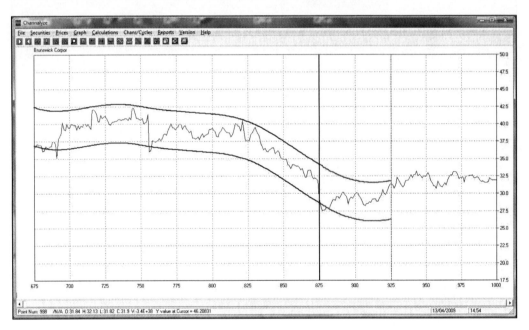

It can be seen from Figure 11.5 that the actual turning point was at point 903, on 21 August. When it is considered that the gap between the last calculated point and the last data point is 50 days, then to estimate the turning point of the channel (and hence the average) to within nine days of the correct value is a vindication of this method of analysing the relationship between the data and the channel.

Figure 11.5 – The channel drawn once more data was available. The actual bottom was at point 903 (21 August).

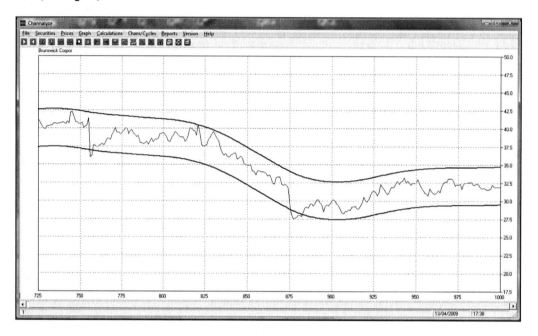

In this type of visual analysis, what we are doing is unconsciously using the properties and relationship of the cycles of wavelength less than the span of the average to modify the position of the cycles of longer wavelength.

To be successful, it is necessary that these cycles of lesser wavelengths should be prominent across the gap that is to be extrapolated. Without this, there will be no features to help in establishing the upper and lower boundaries. The centre section of Figure 11.5 is a case in point. This section is expanded in Figure 11.6. There are no obvious features to help to determine the positions of the upper or lower boundaries. In such a case the only conclusion is that the channel is not about to change direction.

Figure 11.6 – The extrapolated section of the channel from Figure 11.5 shows no features that will help to determine whether the channel has changed direction. It must be assumed that it has not.

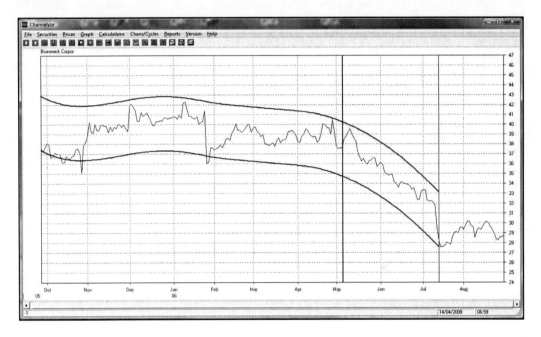

The relationship between the channel we have been discussing and shorter wavelength cycles is shown in Figure 11.7.

Here we have plotted the nominal 15-day cycle. As expected, there is a correlation between those places in the chart where the cycle is prominent, i.e. its amplitude is above the typical value, and those points in the channel where the price touches the boundaries. In order to highlight these touching points, the channel depth has been decreased to contain 92% of the data points instead of 97.5%.

Figure 11.7 – The lower panel shows the nominal cycle of wavelength 15 days in a section of the Brunswick Corporation stock price. It can be seen that those points where the cycle is of higher amplitude are the points in the channel where the stock price approaches the appropriate boundary. The channel depth has been decreased in order to accentuate the channel touching points.

Reducing the channel depth

If there are some fairly prominent features that do not reach a channel boundary, then there is the option of reducing the constant depth of the channel. This is more likely to be required when a large span is used for the underlying average. Thus shown in Figure 11.8 is the channel derived from the 301-point average in the British American Tobacco stock price.

Figure 11.8 – The 301-day channel in British American Tobacco. There are very few touching points in the long upward run until the end of 2007.

The way in which the channel topped out in May 2008 is of interest since, as shown in Figure 11.9, the initial extrapolation of the channel by continuing its rate of curvature seems to fit in with the oscillations of the price data.

Figure 11.9 – The 301-day channel in British American Tobacco. The channel depth has been reduced to allow 10% of the points to lie outside of the boundaries. As a result there are now many more touching points.

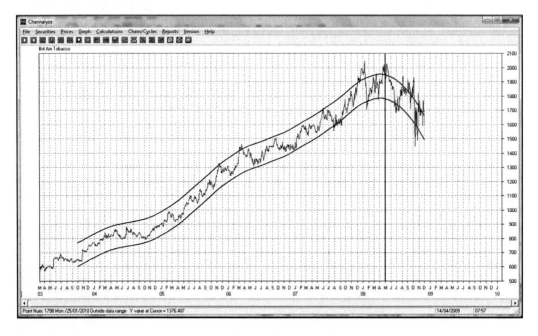

In order to see this more clearly, this section is enlarged in Figure 11.10. Here the channel depth has been set back to its initial value where 3.5% of the data points are allowed to be outside the boundaries.

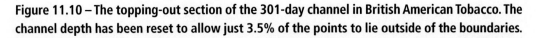

Figure 11.10 – The topping-out section of the 301-day channel in British American Tobacco. The channel depth has been reset to allow just 3.5% of the points to lie outside of the boundaries.

The interesting point about this chart is that there are now five areas (not necessarily a sharp, single peak or trough) where the price either touches or just penetrates the boundary. Comparison with Figure 11.9 shows that the reason is the increased amplitude of shorter-term cycles in this section. Two questions arise from this. Firstly, what is the particular short-term cycle or band of cycles which are now so prominent? Secondly, how far back in time can we move the latest data point and arrive at the fact that the channel is now topping out?

The short-term cycles in British American Tobacco

A rough approximation of the wavelength of the more recent short-term cycles can be obtained by inspection of the peaks and troughs in the extrapolated section of the channel in Figure 11.10. The peaks are about 100 days apart, as are the troughs.

In order to check this, the nominal 101-day cycle is plotted in the lower panel in Figure 11.11. Now the relationship can be seen quite clearly. The amplitude increases from 38p to 90p over this period. As might be expected, the peaks and troughs in the cycle are in line with the peaks and troughs in the data which approach the channel boundaries.

Figure 11.11 – The topping-out section of the 301-day channel in British American Tobacco. The nominal 101-day cycle is shown in the lower panel. The time axis is labelled with numbers so that the wavelength of the cycles can be checked. See text for explanation of vertical lines.

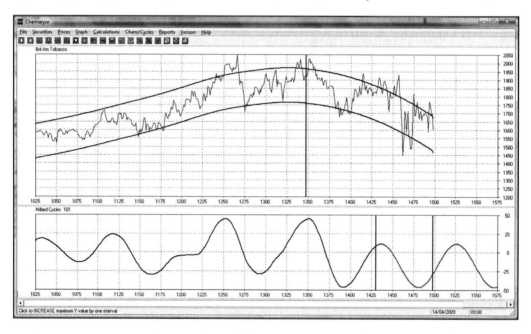

The vertical line in the lower panel of Figure 11.11 shows the position of the last true calculated point of the cycle. The second vertical line in the lower panel represents the latest data point. The vertical line in the upper panel is the start of the extrapolation of the channel. The cycle has been extrapolated into the future.

Predicting whether the turning point has occurred

Figure 11.12 shows the position at 28 May 2008 at point 1365. The initial extrapolation of the upper boundary seems to be perfectly correct, since the peaks at point 1341 (24 April) and point 1352 (9 May) with values of 2023p and 2027p are just touching the upper boundary. There is no reason to expect the channel to do anything other than continue to rise.

Figure 11.12 – The channel extrapolation at 28 May 2008 at point 1365. There is no reason to believe that the channel is topping out.

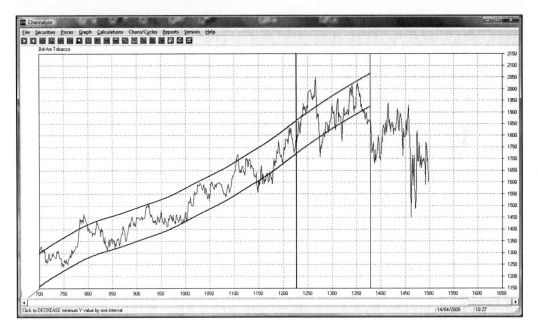

The latest data point at 1365 (28 May) has a value of 1889p and this is just below the lower boundary. It is only slightly below the boundary and so this level of penetration is acceptable.

The position at 18 June is shown in Figure 11.13. The latest price is now well below the lower boundary and there is also a sign that the rate of climb of the channel is decreasing. Since the price is so far below the lower boundary, the channel will have to be adjusted to reduce the amount of penetration.

Figure 11.13 – The channel extrapolation at 18 June 2008 at point 1380. There is now just a suggestion that the rate of climb of the channel is decreasing. The value of the last data point on 18 June is 1831p, which is well below the lower boundary.

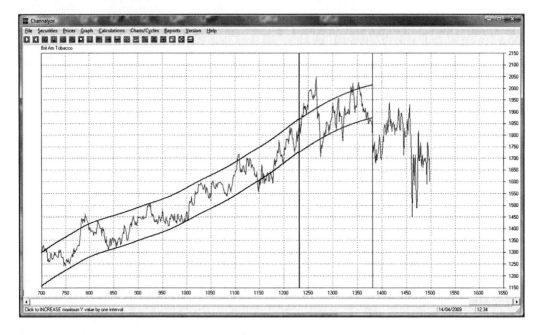

The shape of the channel after an adjustment is shown in Figure 11.14. The adjustment which has been made brings the lower boundary down to the level of the latest point at 1831p. This means that the two peaks at 1341 and 1352 mentioned earlier now penetrate the upper boundary by a considerable amount. However, experience of channel turning points shows that there is almost always an overshoot of boundaries in such cases. Thus in the current circumstances the adjusted position of the channel is acceptable. Therefore we can now see quite clearly that the channel is now topping out.

Figure 11.14 – The channel extrapolation at 18 June 2008 at point 1380 has now been adjusted by increasing the curvature to accommodate the low value (1831p) of the latest data point.

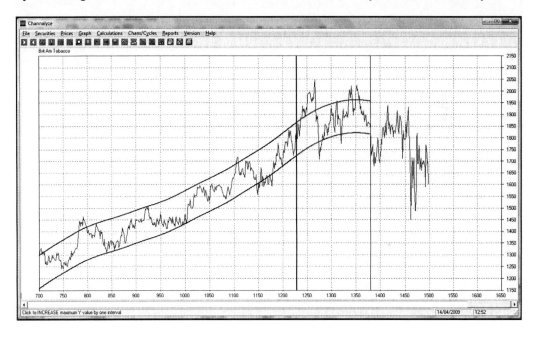

If we move on to point 1399 (15 July), where the value has fallen to 1693p, then we get the position shown in Figure 11.15. The penetration of the upper boundary is now quite large, so an adjustment is needed to attempt to reduce this. The adjusted channel is shown in Figure 11.16.

Figure 11.15 – The channel extrapolation at 15 July 2008 at point 1399. The channel has not been adjusted, but the fact that it has topped out is obvious.

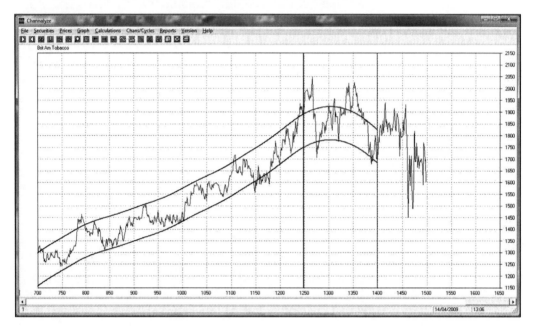

Figure 11.16 – The channel extrapolation at 15 July 2008 at point 1399. The channel has now been adjusted in order to try to reduce the penetration of the upper boundaries.

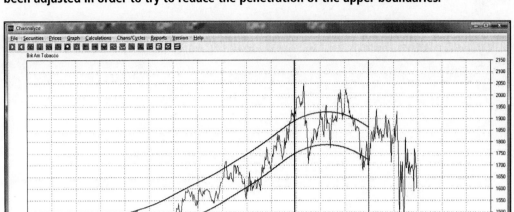

If we now look at the channel from the point of view of exactly where we have found the topping point to be, then this point is about halfway across the gap, with its maximum at around point 1308 on 10 March 2008. Thus we have been able to establish that the channel, and hence the average upon which it is based, topped out some four months in the past.

That this estimate of the position of the top of the channel is correct can be seen from a plot of the channel once sufficient data had arrived for its calculation. This is shown in Figure 11.17. The actual channel top occurred at point 1326 on 3 April 2008. Although this is some 18 days later than predicted by the channel analysis, it should be pointed out that since we are using a 301-point average, the gap is half a span, i.e. 150 days wide. An error of 18 days in 150 days is more than acceptable in warning that the current direction of the long-term trend is now downwards.

Figure 11.17 – A later calculation enables the exact top to be determined at point 1326 (3 April 2008) as shown by the arrow.

Predicting if the turning point will occur in the near future

It would be even more useful if we could use this method of analysis to determine whether the channel was about to change direction in the near future. However, this is quite difficult for channels based on a high value for the period of the average, such as the 301 days that we have used in the previous examples. It will not work if we have a gradual increase in the amplitude of the shorter-term cycles contained within the channel. This is because in such a case there is probably a prominent cycle about to develop over the near future that is not yet part of the calculation and so will have a large effect once it is included in the near future.

Thus the most likely scenario to give an indication of a change of direction in the near future is where successive peaks are aligned with the upper boundary. An example can be seen in Figure 11.18 for the H.J. Heinz Company. The last data point is at 20 February 2007 with a value of $47.69.

Figure 11.18 – At this time in the H.J. Heinz Company stock price (point 1034 (20 February 2007, $47.69)) it is predicted that the channel will top out in the near future.

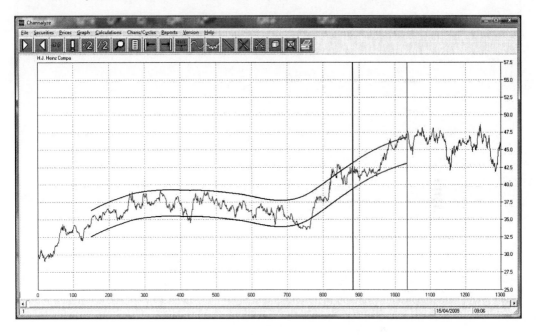

The indication is that the channel is showing a decreasing rate of climb and should top out somewhere in the future. Only a slight adjustment is needed to align the upper boundary with the recent peaks, as shown in Figure 11.19.

Figure 11.19 – A small adjustment has been made to bring the upper boundary to the level of the recent peaks.

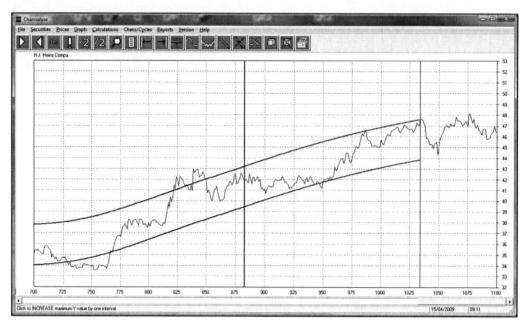

The indication is still that the channel will top out in the near future and the estimation by extrapolating the current amount of curvature is that this will happen by the time the right hand end of the chart is reached, around point 1100.

As shown in Figure 11.20, the actual top of the channel occurred at the point indicated by the arrow, point 1106 on 31 May 2008. Our estimation of topping out, although rough and ready since it is based on extrapolating the curve of the channel into the future, was therefore very helpful. Since the price was at the upper boundary, the decision would be taken to sell, since the probability is high of a rebound back towards the centre of the channel.

Figure 11.20 – A later calculation enables the exact top to be determined, point 1106 (31 May 2008) as shown by the arrow.

Rising or falling?

An interesting chart is that of the British pound vs US dollar, as shown in Figure 11.21, with the latest data point being at point 770 on 12 February 2006. It is interesting because, unlike the previous examples in which the short-term cycles contained within the channel were either of fairly constant amplitude or increasing in amplitude, it can be seen in Figure 11.21 that the short-term cycles have diminished greatly. Even so, the indication is quite obvious that the channel has already bottomed out, with a turning point at about point 718 on 1 December. Notice the long gap from May 2005 until the latest point where there is no close approach to the upper boundary. It is the sequence of troughs from July 2005 that have defined the lower boundary and, hence, by virtue of the constant channel depth, also the upper boundary.

Figure 11.21 – The 301-day channel in a chart of the British pound/US dollar with the last data point at point 770 on 12 February 2006. The indication is that the channel bottomed out around point 718 on 1 December 2005.

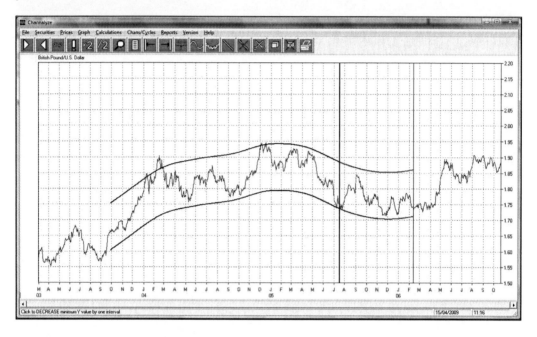

A few weeks later, the newly calculated channel appeared as shown in Figure 11.22. Now the bend has disappeared and the indication is for a falling channel. A close inspection shows that the lower boundary has now moved away from the succession of troughs that had defined it on the earlier occasion. It can be seen that the channel can be adjusted so that these troughs are at the lower boundary without causing a difficulty with the peaks in this region.

Figure 11.22 – The 301-day channel in the chart of the British pound/US dollar with the last data point at point 794 on 17 March 2006. The extrapolated channel has now straightened out with no indication of a turn having occurred at around point 718 (1 December 2005).

The adjustment which causes the channel to bend upwards is shown in Figure 11.23.

Figure 11.23 – The 301-day channel in the chart of the British pound/US dollar has now been adjusted to bring the recent troughs to the lower boundary.

It could also be argued, if not quite as convincingly, that the channel could be adjusted downwards, so that the bunch of small peaks around point 750 could sit on the upper boundary. This is shown in Figure 11.24. However, the fact that the data itself is trending sideways would perhaps suggest that the fall in the channel is becoming less steep.

Figure 11.24 – The 301-day channel in the chart of the British pound/US dollar has now been adjusted to bring the recent peaks to the upper boundary.

This ambiguous situation is one in which no decision can yet be taken about the future path of the 301-day channel. If raising the boundary is the correct view to take, then we would expect the price to rebound upwards from this adjusted lower boundary.

If lowering the boundary is the correct view, then we would expect the price to rebound downwards back from this upper boundary. To solve this dilemma it is simply necessary to wait for a few more days until the situation becomes resolved. Never try to force a conclusion out of inconclusive data.

Figure 11.25 – The 301-day channel in the chart of the British pound/US dollar as at point 823 on 27 May 2006. The direction of the channel has now been verified as changing from falling to rising. The low point in the channel is at point 764, on 3 March 2006.

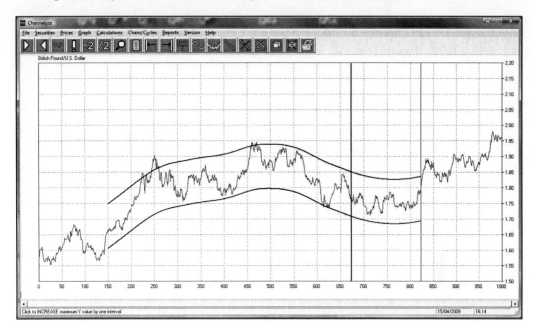

As can be seen in Figure 11.25, the position on 27 May 2006 shows that the channel has bottomed out and is now rising. Since such a long-term channel is involved, it can be expected to continue to rise for some time into the future, giving excellent trading opportunities.

The actual position of the channel as determined much later shows that the estimation of the channel direction shown in Figure 11.25 was correct. This is shown in Figure 11.26. The channel actually bottomed out on 6 December 2005 at point 721, compared with the estimated bottom being on 3 March at point 764. While this is a relatively large discrepancy, it should be pointed out once again that the gap between the last calculated point and the last data point is one of 150 days, so that this error of 43 days represents only about a quarter of the gap.

What is extremely interesting is that the first estimation of the turning point as shown in Figure 11.21 for 12 February gave 1 December as the turn. This is only three days away from the actual value!

Figure 11.26 – Enough new data has arrived to enable the change in direction of the 301-day channel in the chart of the British pound/US dollar to be confirmed. The channel bottomed out at point 721 on 6 December 2005.

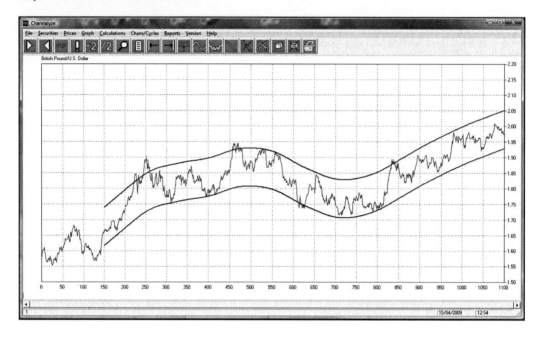

Shorter-term channels

The advantage of using averages with long periods is that they change direction relatively slowly and therefore it is fairly easy to extrapolate the curve across the gap and up to the present time. The disadvantage is, as we have seen, that a long time elapses between the actual turning point and having enough data to be sure that it has turned. Using 301-day channels, this delay amounted to 73 days in the case of British American Tobacco and 59 days in the case of the British pound versus the US dollar.

In the case of the H.J. Heinz Company, there was an indication of the turning point 72 days in advance. However, as was pointed out earlier, it is only on very rare occasions that we are able to do this. Quite clearly, if we reduce the period of the underlying average, we will reduce this time lag, but on the other hand we should expect the extrapolation to the present time to be more difficult.

Multiple channels

It might be thought that channels based on different periods will all top out or bottom out at the same time. However, since channels are based on the sums of cycles this is not the case, since the positions of the peaks and troughs in cycles which are reasonably well separated in wavelengths are independent of each other. For channels, this is illustrated in Figure 11.27.

Figure 11.27 – The topping region of the 301-day channel in the chart of the British Pound versus the US Dollar. Also shown are the 51-day and five-day channels. The channels do not top at the same time. Also note the decreasing smoothness as we move to short periods in the underlying average.

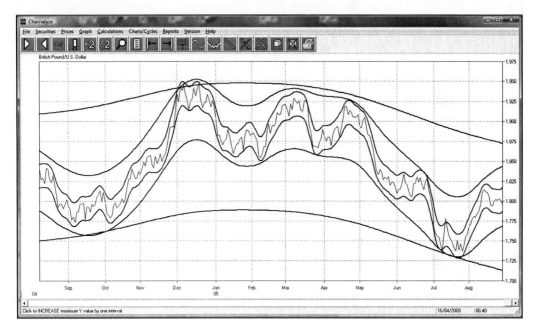

Several important points can be made from a closer look at Figure 11.27:

- the three channels do not top out at the same time

- the smoothness of the channels drops off as we move to smaller values for the underlying period. In the case of the five-day channel, this will make it almost impossible to extrapolate

- what was a single top in the case of the 301-day channel breaks up into multiple tops for the shorter-term channels

- each inner channel bounces off the next outer channel.

Very short-term channels

In Figure 11.28 we show the nine-day channel of the British pound versus the US dollar. This was plotted with the last data point being at point 557 on 20 April 2005. There is no indication in this chart that the rising channel will not continue to rise in the near future.

Figure 11.28 – One of the topping regions of the nine-day channel in the chart of the British pound versus the US dollar. The last data point is at point 557 on 20 April 2005. There is no indication that the channel will be topping out in the near future.

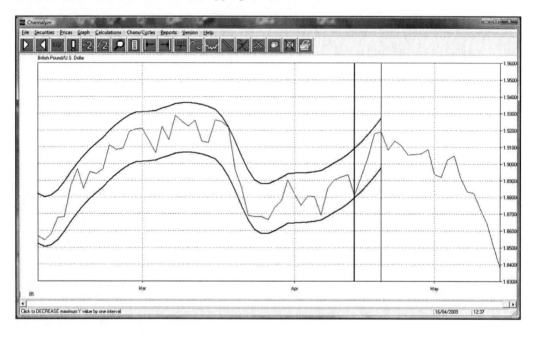

However, a few days later at point 561 on 26 April, as shown in Figure 11.29, we can see that the data has now violated the lower boundary so that the channel has to be adjusted to take this into account.

Figure 11.29 – Here we show the position a few days later at point 561 on 26 April.

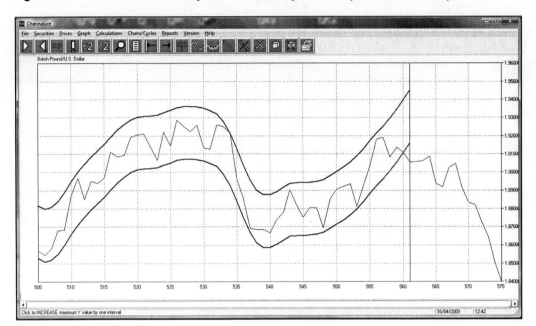

The adjusted channel is shown in Figure 11.30.

Figure 11.30 – Here the channel has been adjusted by raising the lower boundary to accommodate the fact that the data has violated the latter.

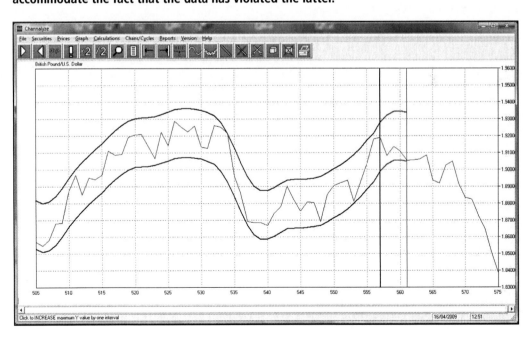

The message from Figures 11.28 to 11.30 is that when short-term channels are used to aid trading decisions, the position can change very quickly. Usually it is not possible to decide that a channel has changed direction until we reach a situation where the latest data point violates the boundary, making it necessary to carry out an adjustment. More often than not, this adjustment will generate a bend in the channel so that it can be seen to have topped out or bottomed out.

However, if the data is inspected closely, a warning sign that the price itself may reverse direction is given by the relationship between the price and a boundary. In the case of a rising channel such as that shown in Figure 11.28, it can be seen that the peak value at point 556 on 19 April is very close to the upper boundary. Thus the trader would expect the price to fall at this point since it is in a low probability area for maintaining its position.

The main difficulty with short-term channels is that the price movements contained within them, since they are of such a short-term nature, do not give the range of movement that can be seen with longer-term channels. There is therefore a happy medium in which the delay in determining that a channel has changed direction can be balanced against the potential for a large rise or fall.

This chapter has covered the analysis of the channel in order to establish whether it has changed direction or not, and hence establish whether the trend represented by the channel has changed direction.

The issue of the behaviour of the data within the channel, which means an analysis of the short-term trends represented by the intra-channel movement, is covered in the next chapter. It will be seen that the best way of determining whether the short-term trends have changed direction is to establish their nearness to a channel boundary, rather than try to analyse channels based on the extrapolation of short-term centred averages, which is not recommended.

12

Trend Turning Points (III)

In the last chapter we saw that by careful analysis, using the peaks and troughs contained within a channel, we could establish whether the channel had changed direction in the gap between the latest data point and the last calculated point for the underlying centred average. This analysis usually entailed an adjustment to the curvature of the extrapolated boundaries. We also saw that when it came to channels based on very short-term averages, this method of extrapolation became more difficult because the averages were no longer smooth, owing to the influence of very short-term cycles. They also changed direction very quickly.

Here we will be investigating the behaviour of the intra-channel movements of the data. Since these reflect the behaviour of the sums of all the cycles of wavelength less than the period used for the average, then by using an underlying average of much shorter than the 301-days used in the last chapter, we can study these short-term trends and attempt to decide whether these have changed direction. A useful value for the average is one of 51 days. This value is the divider between cycles of wavelength greater that 51 days (this forms the channel itself) and those of wavelength equal to or less than 51 days (the intra-channel movement). Since cycles spend half of their time rising (these are uptrends) and half of their time falling (these are downtrends), then the intra-channel trends for a 51-day channel will be those of a persistence of 25 days or less.

In Figure 12.1 we show the chart of Safeway Inc. with the 51-day channel superimposed. The most striking point is on how many occasions the intra-channel movement took the price to the boundaries, from which the price then retreated.

Figure 12.1 – The 51-day channel for Safeway Inc. Note the large number of occasions in which the price movement reached the channel boundaries.

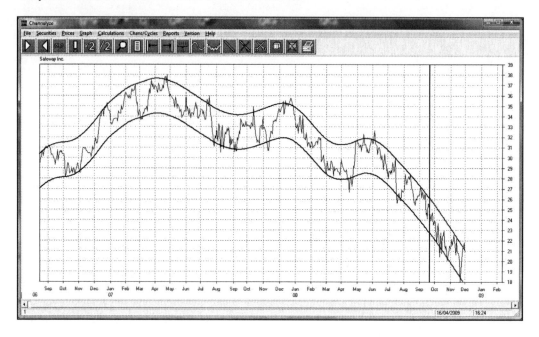

A rising section of the Safeway chart is shown in Figure 12.2. Here the points of contact or near contact have been circled. The short-term movements are responsible for quite useful percentage changes.

Figure 12.2 – The 51-day channel for Safeway Inc. The occasions in which the price movement reached the rising channel boundaries have been circled.

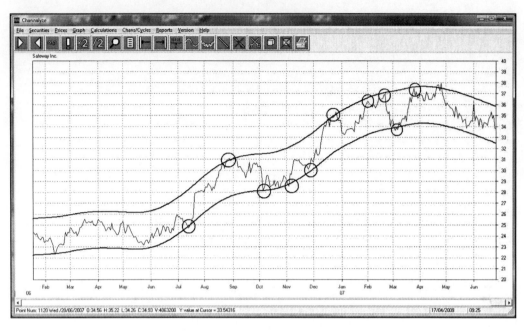

The price ranges covered by the bottom-to-top channel movements are shown in Table 12.1.

Table 12.1 – The data from three bottom-to-top channel rises in Safeway Inc. stock. The 51-day channel is rising.

Date	Value ($)	Top/Bottom	Percent rise	Days
13 Jul 2006	24.75	Bottom		
28 Aug 2006	31.01	Top	25.3	32
27 Nov 2006	30.09	Bottom		
18 Dec 2006	34.61	Top	15	15
5 Mar 2007	33.66	Bottom		
26 Mar 2007	37.52	Top	11.5	15

These movements are obviously not derived from just one cycle. If they had been, then since the wavelength would be constant, the times taken for the rises would all be equal. It can be seen in Table 12.1 that they are not, two taking 15 days and one taking 32 days. We will see in the next chapter which short-term cycles were present at this particular time in the chart of Safeway Inc.

Having seen how these movements have been identified with the benefit of hindsight, it is necessary to see how we would have identified them at the time that they were happening.

Rising channel

The sequence of events shown in Figures 12.3 to 12.6 shows how the analysis proceeds for Safeway during the latter part of 2006. There is always a logical sequence to follow:

1. draw extrapolated channel

2. check for price penetration of either boundary

3. if there is price penetration of either boundary, adjust channel

4. if price is at a lower boundary, wait for trough to be formed to confirm boundary position before trading

5. if price is at an upper boundary, wait for peak to be formed to confirm boundary position before trading.

It is important that this procedure be repeated each day, as the new closing price must be used in the re-calculation of the underlying average.

Safeway, 7 November 2006

The calculation of the 51-day channel gives the extrapolation shown in Figure 12.3. While the extrapolated portion shows a downward curve which has topped out in the gap, it is quite clear that the latest price is now rising above the upper boundary.

Figure 12.3 – The 51-day channel for Safeway Inc. The price on 7 November 2006 ($29.6) is now penetrating the upper boundary. The channel therefore needs to be adjusted upwards.

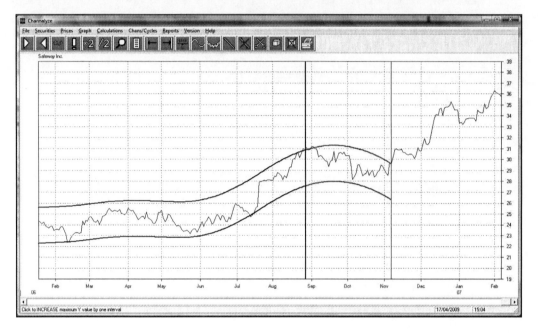

An adjustment is therefore necessary to lift the curve so that the penetration disappears – this is shown in Figure 12.4. The result is that the adjusted channel is running essentially sideways. The fact that there is a succession of small troughs adds extra validity to the new position of the lower boundary and gives confidence that there will be a rise from this position, since we are now in an area of low probability of the price remaining at this location.

Figure 12.4 – The 51-day channel for Safeway Inc. The channel in Figure 12.3 has now been adjusted to give a sideways direction.

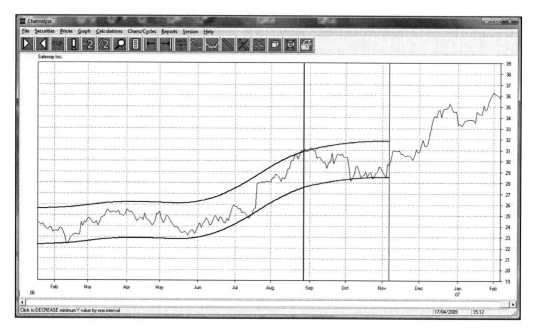

Safeway, 29 November 2006

By 29 November the extrapolated channel appears as in Figure 12.5. We now have the reverse situation, where the price on 29 November is violating the upper boundary of the channel. An adjustment is therefore necessary to remove this penetration. It would be premature to assume that this is the extent of the current rise until the channel has been adjusted.

Figure 12.5 – The 51-day channel for Safeway Inc. The channel was calculated on 29 November 2006 with the price at $30.5. The price is now violating the upper boundary again. The channel therefore needs to be adjusted upwards.

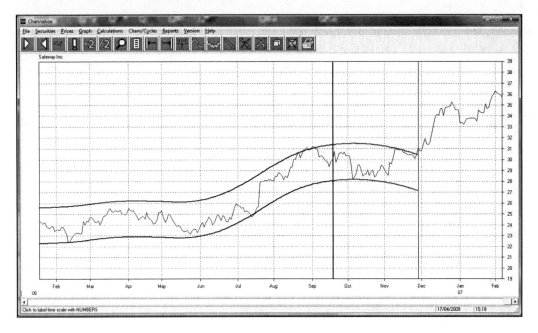

The adjusted channel is shown in Figure 12.6. A large adjustment has been made here since this brings the sequence of small troughs mentioned above and the new small trough formed between the 27 and 29 November to the lower boundary.

Figure 12.6 – The 51-day channel for Safeway Inc. The channel in Figure 12.5 has now been adjusted to give an upwards direction. The small trough two days previously on 27 November identifies the position of the lower boundary.

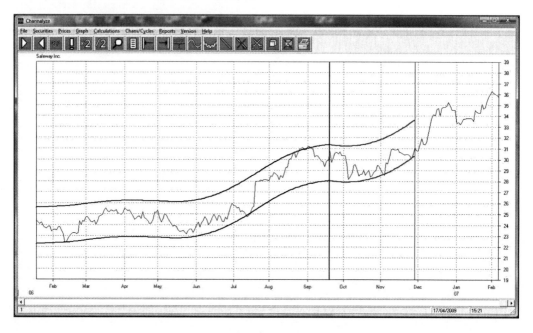

If there hadn't been a small trough at this point then the boundary would not be raised as far and a few more days would need to be allowed to pass before the situation was clarified. A trade placed on 7 November would still be in place awaiting a significant rebound downwards.

Safeway, 18 December 2006

By 18 December 2006 the price, at $34.61, had penetrated the upper boundary, as shown in Figure 12.7. Whether the stock should be sold at this point cannot be decided, since the first step is to adjust the channel to remove this penetration of the upper boundary. Once this adjustment is carried out, then whether to sell or not will depend upon whether the price movement forms a peak or not. If no peak is formed, then it should not be sold.

Figure 12.7 – The position of the extrapolated channel on 18 December 2006. The price is at $34.61 and violates the upper boundary. This will need an adjustment to remove the overlap.

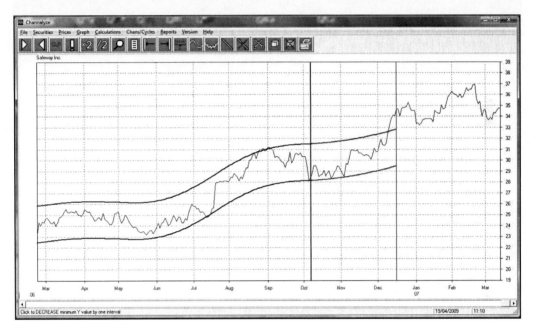

The result of adjusting the boundary is shown in Figure 12.8. Subsequently the price fell back to $34 on 20 December, which would be the signal to sell. Perversely, of course, the price moved back up again to peak out at $35.31 on 27 December. Although a small amount of extra profit was lost, to sell a few days earlier was the correct decision.

Figure 12.8 – The 51-day channel for Safeway Inc. has now been adjusted to remove the violation of the upper boundary.

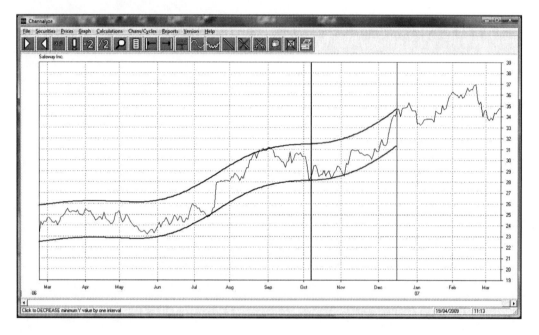

Safeway, 27 April 2007

The extrapolated channel drawn for Safeway on 27 April is shown in Figure 12.9. The extrapolated portion has now topped out, but it can be seen that the latest peak is violating the upper boundary. This means that it needs to be adjusted and of course the adjustment may remove the bend from the extrapolated portion.

Figure 12.9 – The 51-day channel for Safeway Inc. calculated on 27 April 2007. The extrapolated channel appears to have topped out but still needs an adjustment.

The adjusted channel is shown in Figure 12.10 and it can be seen that even after this necessary adjustment, the channel is still topping out. It is now time to close out the position.

Figure 12.10 – The 51-day channel for Safeway Inc. calculated on 27 April 2007 has now been adjusted to remove the violation by the latest price on 27 April.

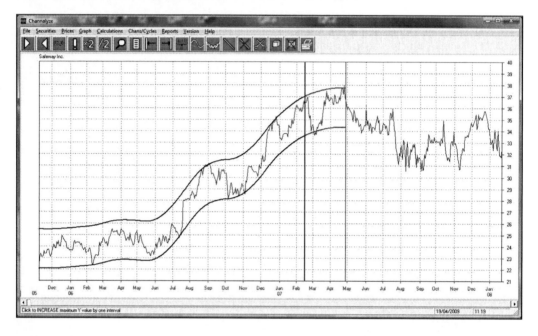

This has been a useful exercise in extrapolating and checking if an adjustment is needed over this whole upward trend, and the value of a careful analysis has been shown.

While there is always a temptation to jump the gun in buying situations and a temptation to wait a little longer on selling situations, these temptations must be avoided if a successful trading strategy is to be maintained.

Part of the reason for jumping the gun is that the trader feels that a lot of profit can be lost by waiting. What should be balanced against this is the increased risk of things going wrong. It can be seen from this example that there is still plenty of profit in each cross-channel rise even if the rises over the first and last days of the trend are removed.

Falling channel

The profit to be obtained from the trends within a falling 51-day channel will be less than those from a rising channel, because the price rise will reach the upper boundary which is already falling. The amount by which it falls over the period during which the short-term trend is rising is obviously reducing the extent of the rise in the short-term trend. On the other hand, the falls will be greater.

The chart for AstraZeneca shown in Figure 12.11 is a good example of a great many intra-channel rises and falls which reach the upper and lower boundaries of the channel.

Figure 12.11 – The 51-day channel for AstraZeneca. Note the large number of occasions in which the price movement reached the channel boundaries.

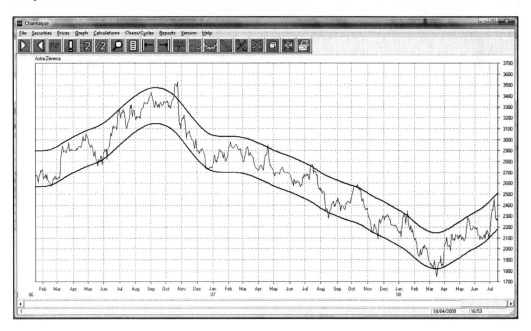

As far as the intra-channel movements are concerned during a period in which the channel undergoes a sustained fall, these are illustrated in Figure 12.12. Here the points at which the price movement approaches the upper and lower boundaries have been circled for ease of recognition.

Figure 12.12 – The 51-day channel for AstraZeneca. The occasions in which the price movement reached the falling channel boundaries have been circled.

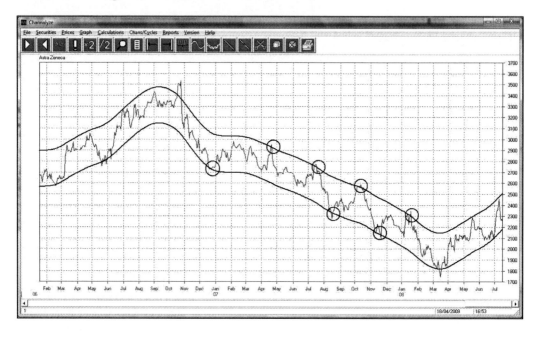

The range of movement for three of these intra-channel excursions is shown in Table 12.2.

Table 12.2 – The data from three bottom-to-top channel falls in AstraZeneca stock. The 51-day channel is falling.

Date	Value (p)	Top/Bottom	Per cent fall	Days
16 Jul 2007	2770	Top		
4 Oct 2007	2570	Top		
9 Nov 2007	2146	Bottom	16.5	21
18 Jan 2008	2345	Top		
11 Feb 2008	1929	Bottom	17.7	16

In Figures 12.13 to 12.22 we investigate how the channel position would be estimated from the same procedure as we used for Safeway, i.e. extrapolate the channel and then check whether an adjustment is needed in the light of the latest value for the data.

AstraZeneca, 3 January 2007

The position of the extrapolated channel for 3 January 2007 is shown in Figure 12.13. Quite obviously the last few data points are well above the channel and hence the channel will need to be adjusted in order to remove the degree of penetration. While the extrapolation shows the channel to have topped out, it can be seen that an adjustment might cause the channel to move sideways or even to continue to rise.

Figure 12.13 – The 51-day channel for AstraZeneca on 3 January 2007. The channel will need to be adjusted since the latest price is well above the upper boundary.

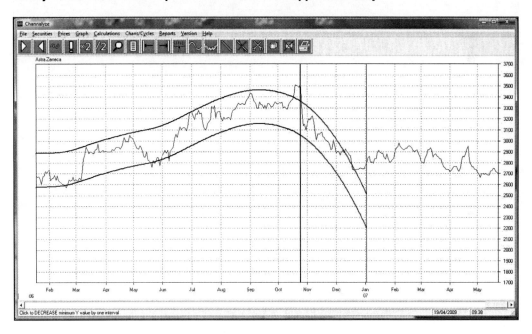

The adjusted channel is shown in Figure 12.14. It was not possible to remove the penetration of the peak in late October. Since on most occasions where a channel tops out there is an overshoot of the data above the upper boundary, this was accepted as being the case in this example.

Figure 12.14 – The 51-day channel for AstraZeneca on 3 January 2007. The channel has been adjusted to bring the latest price (2787p) to the lower boundary. The penetration by the peak in late October cannot be removed by channel bending so it is accepted as a normal overshoot at a channel top.

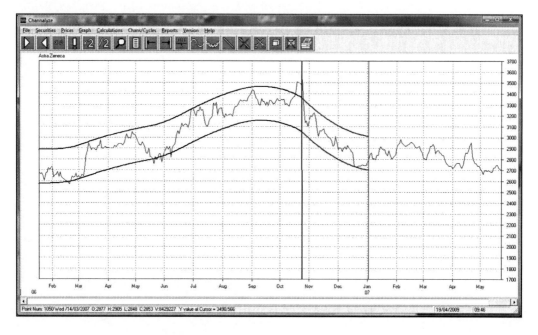

There was also the decision as to whether to lower the channel slightly so as to bring the latest price to the upper boundary, or to lower it by a larger amount and bring the trough just formed to the lower boundary. Since troughs are more often associated with lower boundaries, this appears to be the best approach in the current circumstances. However, in cases like this where there is a credible alternative to the placement of the channel boundaries, no decision about placing a trade should be made until the situation is clarified by the new data points arriving over the next few days.

AstraZeneca, 7 February 2007

The position at 7 February 2007 is shown in Figure 12.15. Here the price at 2950p is now above the extrapolated boundary. Thus an adjustment will have to be made.

Figure 12.15 – The 51-day channel for AstraZeneca on 7 February 2007. The price is at 2950p and is above the extrapolated boundary.

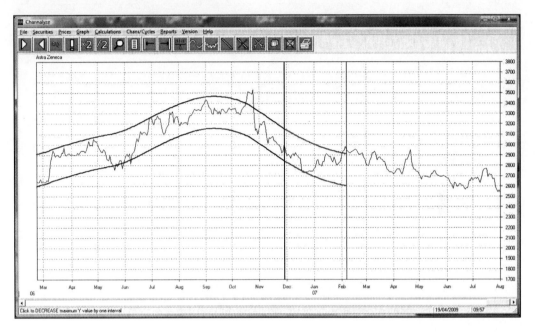

The adjustment is shown in Figure 12.16. As can be seen, only a small lift in the position of the channel is necessary to bring the price down to the upper boundary. There is now an indication that the channel is straightening out, but confirmation of this will have to wait for the arrival of more data points over the next few days.

Figure 12.16 – The 51-day channel for AstraZeneca on 7 February 2007 has now been adjusted.

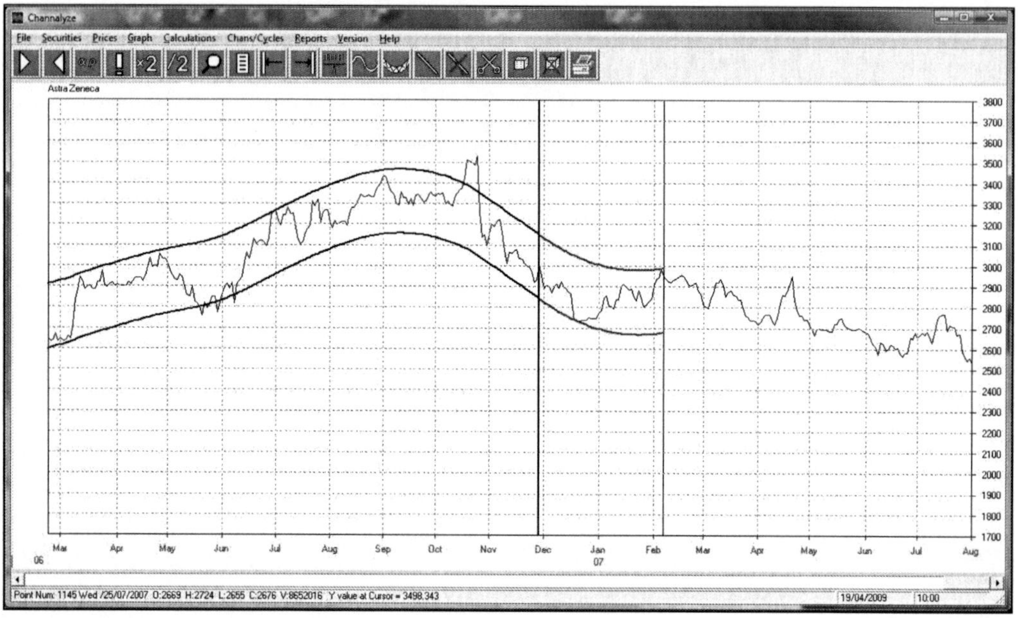

No such conformation was forthcoming and the channel resumed its downwards path as a result of the general trend of price movement being down.

AstraZeneca, 20 August 2007

By 20 August 2007, the position was that shown in Figure 12.17. No adjustment is necessary and the expectation is for a rise in price within the next day or two. This is indeed what happened.

Figure 12.17 – The 51-day channel for AstraZeneca on 20 August 2007. No adjustment is necessary.

AstraZeneca, 16 October 2007

The channel then continued to fall for another few months, until the position shown in Figure 12.18 was reached on 16 October 2007. The price has now risen to the top of the falling channel. Thus a retraction in price is to be expected.

Figure 12.18 – The 51-day channel for AstraZeneca on 16 October 2007. No adjustment is necessary.

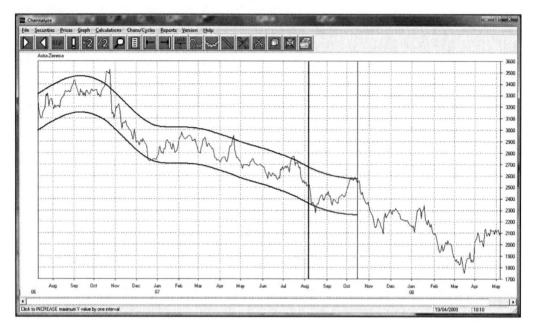

AstraZeneca, 14 November 2007

This position on 14 November 2007 is shown in Figure 12.19. The channel has continued to fall and the small trough formed on 11 November is now almost exactly on the lower boundary. Thus no further adjustment is necessary. The assumption is now that the price will rebound from the lower boundary.

Figure 12.19 – The 51-day channel for AstraZeneca on 14 November 2007. No adjustment is necessary.

AstraZeneca, 16 November 2007

However, two days later the price fell slightly below the boundary and then rose again to form a second trough. This is shown in Figure 12.20. However, the calculation of the extrapolated channel causes it to be in a slightly lower position. This new position puts the second trough on the lower boundary, so no further adjustment is needed.

Figure 12.20 – The 51-day channel for AstraZeneca two days later on 16 November 2007. No adjustment is necessary to accommodate the new trough.

AstraZeneca, 14 January 2008

The position on 14 January 2008 is shown in Figure 12.21. The extrapolated channel has now increased its rate of fall. However, this now causes the peak formed on 11 January to be well above this boundary. The channel needs to be adjusted to remove this violation.

Figure 12.21 – The 51-day channel for AstraZeneca on 14 January 2008 with the price at 2308p. An adjustment is necessary to remove the upper boundary violation on 11 January, when the price was at 2318p.

The adjusted channel is shown in Figure 12.22. This new position for the channel simply continues the downward path of the channel at the same rate of fall that we saw on 16 November.

Figure 12.22 – The 51-day channel for AstraZeneca on 14 January 2008. The adjustment has now been carried out.

AstraZeneca, 20 March 2008

The position on 20 Match 2008 is shown in Figure 12.23. The recent trough on 17 March lies exactly on the lower boundary. This means that no adjustment is necessary.

Figure 12.23 – The 51-day channel for AstraZeneca on 20 March 2008. The price, at 1879p, has risen from the trough at 1748 on 17 March. No adjustment is necessary since this trough lies exactly on the lower boundary.

AstraZeneca, 19 May 2008

The position on 19 March 2008 is shown in Figure 12.24. The extrapolated channel has now bottomed out as a result of the rising short-term trend from the low point. Although the channel has obviously bottomed out, the extrapolation does not look quite right. This is for two reasons. Firstly, channels tend to be approaching symmetry at turning points, i.e. the rate of fall or rise before the turning point is fairly similar to the rate of rise or fall after the turn. This is clearly not the case here. Secondly, the price is staying within the middle of the channel on the new upward leg.

Figure 12.24 – The 51-day channel for AstraZeneca on 19 May 2008. The price at 2289p is well below the extrapolated upper boundary. Quite clearly the channel has now bottomed out. However, the extrapolated part should be more symmetrical about the low point. An adjustment downwards is required.

Usually around a channel turning point the cycles of shorter wavelength will increase in amplitude and reach or penetrate either boundary, so that the extrapolation needs to be adjusted. This is shown in Figure 12.25. Everything looks good and we can be fairly confident that the channel, and hence the underlying 51-day average, has changed direction and is now rising.

Figure 12.25 – The 51-day channel for AstraZeneca on 19 May 2008. The channel has now been adjusted so that the high price on this date is at the upper boundary. It can be seen that the turning point is now much more symmetrical.

It can be seen from the examples that have been presented that on some occasions no adjustment is necessary, since the features in the price movement which help to establish the channel boundaries are all in the right relative positions to the boundaries. The extrapolated boundaries in channels such as these have the highest validity, i.e. have the greatest probability that their estimated positions are correct.

On the other hand, it is at the channel turning points that the greatest amount of adjustment is required to avoid violations of the boundaries. That there is a greater amount of possible error in boundary placement at these positions is to be expected, since the estimated position of the channel will be that it is continuing in the same direction. It is only the fact that the price is penetrating one or other of the boundaries that gives an indication that the direction is about to change.

Finally, it should be noted that in these two cases of Safeway and AstraZeneca, the rising and falling channels remain in this state for a long period of time, during which there are three or four occasions on which a trade could be placed. These longer-term channels were used so that the procedure for confirming a continuation of direction could be more easily explained.

In general, the persistence of the 51-day averages and hence the derived channel is not as long as this. It is more likely that only two or three trades can be placed between the estimated turning points.

Why Does Channel Analysis Work?

We have seen that we can use the extreme excursions of intra-channel short-term trends to establish the path of the channel itself. The extreme excursions are of course caused by the short-term cycles responsible for the short-term trends reaching their maximum amplitude, or rather the percentage of maximum amplitude allowed by the overlap of data points. This interaction would not be possible if the trends were independent of each other, or rather if the sums of cycles causing these trends were independent of each other. Although as noted previously the wavelengths of the cycles present in each set of market data are independent of each other, the fact remains that the amplitudes are not. This is easily demonstrated by an experiment of taking increasingly large periods for the centred moving average used to construct channels and plotting the resulting channel depths.

The result of doing this is shown in Figure 12.26 for three securities in the London market. Similar results are obtained for other stock, currency and commodity markets.

Figure 12.26 – Cycle sums determined from channel depths plotted for AstraZeneca (AZN), Barclays (BARC) and British American Tobacco (BAT). Quadratic curve fitting routines have been used to show the trends in each security, with a high degree of goodness of fit as can be seen from the R^2.

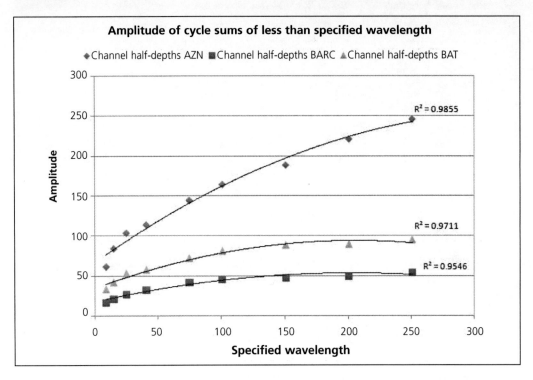

It can be seen quite clearly that the channel depths, which represent the amplitude of the cycle sums contained within each channel, are related to each other as shown by the fitted quadratic curves. The values used in the centred moving average were periods of nine, 15, 25, 41, 75, 101, 151, 201 and 251 days. This covers a sufficient range of cycle wavelengths that the conclusions drawn from the study are perfectly valid.

Since the cycle sums are interactive from the perspective of their amplitudes, two of these are shown in Figure 12.27 to enable their relationship to be discussed. The two averages are 41-day and 75-day centred averages. For all the reasons discussed throughout this book these are presented as centred averages. As such, the fact that the shorter-term averages oscillate around longer-term averages is obvious. If the averages are presented with no lag, then this relationship is lost.

Figure 12.27 – This shows the 41-day and 75-day centred moving averages of AstraZeneca data. The oscillations of the shorter 41-day average around the longer 75-day average are limited by the relationship between them shown in Figure 12.26.

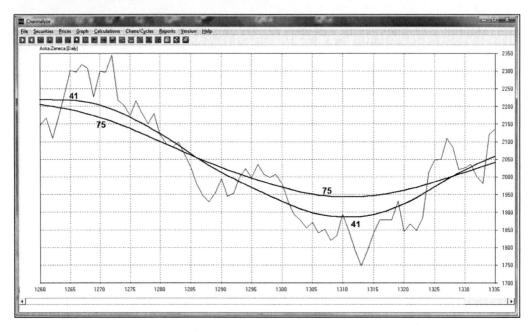

As shown in Figure 12.27, just as was the case with the actual stock data oscillating around a centred average, there is a limit to the extent to which short-term averages oscillate around longer-term averages. Thus the two averages are interactive, so that a change in the amplitude of one average and hence its vertical position at a point in time must be compensated by a change in amplitude and hence the vertical position of the other average. Of course, when the term 'average' is used, what is really meant is the trend for which that particular average is a proxy, which also means the sums of cycles with wavelengths less than the period of the average.

So far, this discussion has only concerned the oscillation of two averages around each other. As can be seen from Figure 12.26, most securities will contain many sums of cycles, so that we can arrive at a very complex situation. However, the complex situation is characterised by a very simple proposition – a change in the amplitude of one cycle so as to take it towards its maximum amplitude will cause all other cycles to change position.

Which are the dominant cycles?

Is it the shorter-term cycles?

In Chapter 11 we saw how using the extremes of the intra-channel cycle sum enabled us to determine the position of the channel boundary and hence the position of the longer-term trend represented by the period used for the average from which the channel was constructed. Thus the cycles of shorter wavelengths have resulted in an adjustment of the cycles of longer wavelength. The conclusion is therefore *Yes!*

Is it the longer-term cycles?

In the earlier part of this chapter we saw that determining the position of the channel boundaries enabled us to determine turning points in the intra-channel cycle sum. Thus the cycles of longer wavelength have modified the position of the peaks and troughs in the cycles of shorter wavelength. The conclusion is therefore *Yes!*

Although in my earlier books on channel analysis I addressed the concept of dominant channels, the above conclusions would indicate that it is not correct to take this view. The interaction between all cycles and cycle sums means that any cycle can be dominant in the sense that if it changes, it will force a change on all other cycles, however small.

If a choice has to be made as to whether short-term or longer-term cycles instigate such a change, then it could be argued that the short-term are the more likely. This is because bad news for a company will manifest itself in an instant response in its stock price. Since this is a short-term response, short-term cycles will react sooner than long-term cycles.

Readers will have their own views. In a sense, though, which of the cycles present in the security is responsible is irrelevant. What is relevant is to use the information to perform the best analysis possible on the implications for the position of a channel and the intra-channel movement.

13

Cycles and Sums of Cycles

We discussed the properties of cycles and how they appeared in market data in Chapter 6. It was clear that market cycles are constantly changing in amplitude, wavelength and phase, going through periods when a nominal cycle is reasonably stable and longer periods when it is not. It was also shown that a cycle only remains stable for around three to five complete sweeps, after which it reverts to its unstable behaviour.

The phrase 'reasonably stable' is used because we will never see a situation in which the amplitude and wavelength remain virtually constant for the duration of these three to five complete sweeps. We will have to limit ourselves to an allowable variation in these parameters, otherwise we will make no progress in our attempt to use market cycles in a predictive sense.

A good starting point where we would expect cycles to remain reasonably stable is the two stocks studied in Chapter 12, where the 51-day channels continued in the same direction for quite a long period of time.

Figure 13.1 shows the distribution of stable cycles in AstraZeneca. These are the cycles present in the historical data for the last five years. It can be seen that the most persistent cycle is the one around the middle of the chart and this has a wavelength of 86 days. There is also a group of shorter wavelength cycles with wavelengths between 11 and 37 days. There is also a longer-term cycle with wavelength 156 days.

Figure 13.1 – The distribution of stable cycles in AstraZeneca. The most persistent cycle is that with wavelength 86 days.

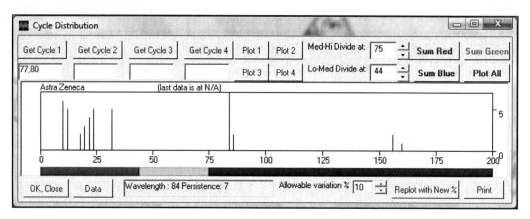

If the sum of the short-term cycles is plotted at the same time as the 101-day channel, as shown in Figure 13.2, we can see that the peaks and troughs in these cycles are aligned perfectly with the touching points in the 101-day channel shown in the upper panel. We use this value of 101 rather than the 51 used in the previous chapter to enable cycles of wavelength 86 days to be studied as intra-channel cycles.

Figure 13.2 – The sum of the short-term stable cycles with wavelengths 11 to 37 days in AstraZeneca. Note how the peaks and troughs are aligned with the touching points within the channel.

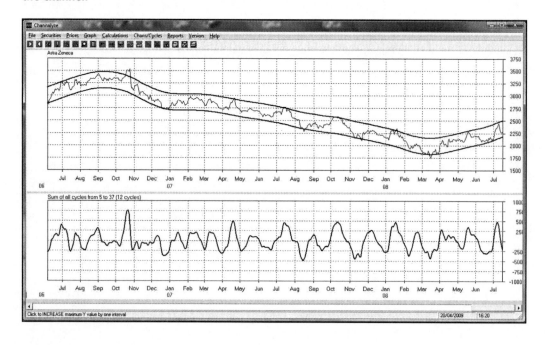

If we take an expanded section of the plot from Figure 13.2, we can see more clearly the relationship between the two (Figure 13.3). The sum of the short-term cycles in the lower panel can now be seen to be much smoother than the intra-channel movement. This is partly because the lower panel does not contain cycles of less than a wavelength of 11 days, while the intra-day movement does. In fact it contains movement down to wavelengths of two days (we will not class one-day movements as cycles). Secondly, not all cycles with wavelengths between 11 days and 37 days are represented in the cycle sum in the lower panel, but only the stable ones whose wavelength and amplitude variation is below the limits of 20%.

Figure 13.3 – An expanded section of the plot from Figure 13.2. It can now be seen that there is much more very short-term random movement within the channel. The extrapolated part of the channel is that to the right of the vertical line in the upper panel. The extrapolated part of the cycle sum is that to the right of the vertical line in the lower panel.

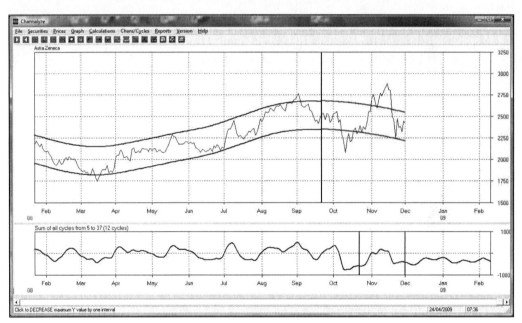

Extrapolation of Cycles

Note that just as is the case with channels, the cycle calculation terminates in the past. The higher the wavelength of the cycle, the further back is the last true calculated point and the longer the extrapolation. In the case of a cycle sum, the extrapolation is that needed for cycles of longest wavelength. Thus in Figure 13.3 this extrapolation is shown as being from a point in late October. This is a very important point, because it will be seen in later examples that the calculation of cycle sums can give an astonishingly accurate estimation of the path of a trend over long periods of time.

To provide a better comparison between the intra-channel movement and this cycle sum it is necessary to smooth out the intra-channel movement by removing cycles of less than 11-day wavelength. This is done by using a nine-point centred average (an 11-point average would remove cycles of wavelength 11 days, which is not what we want to happen). For ease of comparison, the price data itself is removed from the plot shown in Figure 13.4.

Figure 13.4 – The intra-channel movement has now been smoothed by using a nine-point centred average. The actual price data has been removed to aid the comparison with the cycle sum in the lower panel.

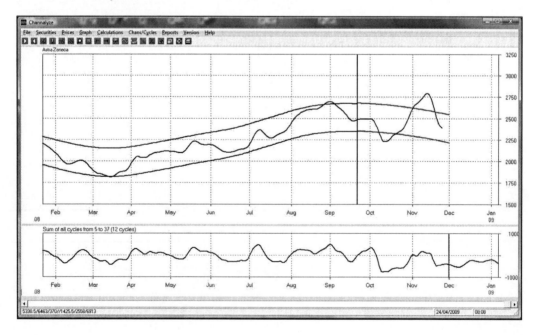

It can now be seen that up to the extrapolated part of the channel, the cycle sum and the nine-point average are very similar. However, there is a difference between these two over the last section of the plot. Why is this?

The answer lies in the fact that the properties of moving averages mean that the intra-channel movement in the case of this 101-day channel is the sum of all cycles of wavelength 101 days or less. We have left out an important cycle from the cycle sum and that is the cycle of wavelength 84 days. This cycle is shown in Figure 13.5

Figure 13.5 – The cycle of wavelength 84 days is shown in the lower panel. The peaks and troughs are mostly aligned with the major touching points in the channel.

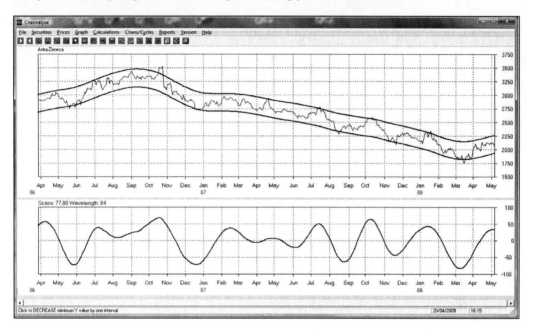

The peaks and troughs in this cycle are mostly aligned with the major touching points of the intra-channel movement. However, it should be noted that this cycle is present in the distribution plot shown in Figure 13.1 because it is stable when determined at the position of the latest data point, which is further on in time than the position shown in Figure 13.5. Thus between April 2006 and July 2007 the cycle is obviously in an unstable state, while from July 2007 onwards it is in a more stable state. If the distribution had been determined in early July 2007, this cycle would not have appeared. Only those cycles which are currently stable at the time that the distribution is determined are isolated.

Now we can see how a plot of all cycles from wavelengths 11 to 84 will compare with the nine-point centred average. This is shown in Figure 13.6.

Figure 13.6 – The cycle sum in the lower panel now contains all cycles of wavelengths up to 96 days.

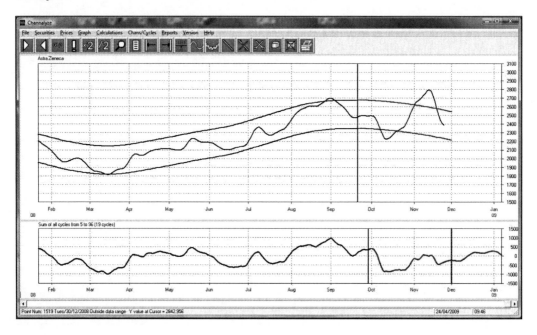

There is a reasonable fit between the cycle sum and the nine-point average until a point about a third of the way along the extrapolated portion of the cycle sum. Then we can see that the cycle sum has bottomed out at a point when the nine-point average is still falling. The average is of course terminating half of its span in the past, but even allowing for that, these two plots are now out of synchronisation.

If we take the sum of all of the cycles up to a wavelength of 300 days we get the position shown in Figure 13.7. Because of the large gap which has to be filled by extrapolation of these large wavelengths, this extrapolation covers almost all of the plot shown in the figure. Even so, it can be seen that there is a good comparison between the extrapolated values and the actual intra-channel movement.

Figure 13.7 – The cycle sum in the lower panel now contains all cycles of wavelengths up to 300 days. Because of this large wavelength, the extrapolation of the cycle sum starting from the first vertical line in the lower panel covers almost all of the plot. Note how good the comparison is over most of the plot until the last few weeks. The vertical line in the upper panel is the start of the extrapolation of the channel.

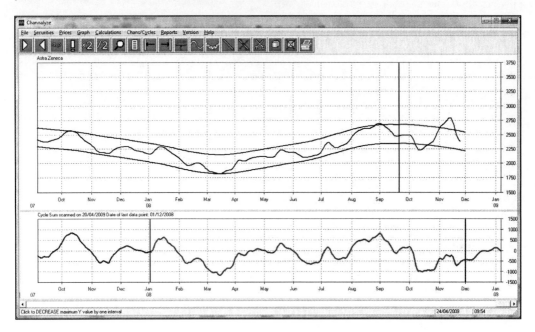

The Comparator

In order to check how reliable a calculation of the cycle sum is as a proxy for the trend, we need to be able to confirm that it is still valid up to as recent a point in the past as possible. We have already used a nine-day centred average to smooth out the very short-term fluctuations in Figures 13.4 to 13.7. The advantage of this particular value is that the gap between the last calculated point and the present time is only four days. Thus if we see our predicted trend is in line with this centred average right up until four days ago, then we have high confidence that it is still valid today and should stay valid for the immediate future. **This is a fundamental issue in using cycle sums for trend prediction.**

Using this approach will rapidly discount those situations where the cycle sum is no longer valid and enable more time to be spent on the analysis of the situations which are valid. **Experience shows that only around 10% of stocks are in a phase where the cycles are currently stable enough to be good predictors of future trend movement.**

213

The comparator is actually the trend which we would like to estimate into the future since, as we showed earlier in this book, the price oscillates about the trend. The shorter the span of the average, the tighter the oscillations around this average. Thus a reasonable restricted range for a future price level will be the result of estimating a future trend based on a nine-day average.

Our daily test, therefore, of the value of using cycle sums is to check the accuracy of the prediction of the nine-day average right up to the point at which it terminates four days back in the past. If this prediction is not accurate, then the future prediction will not be accurate. At some point, the trend and the position of the price relative to the trend will be in a favourable position for the trader to open a position.

There are three reasons why a cycle sum is no longer valid:

1. One or more of the cycles may have changed wavelength and/or amplitude slightly so that the prediction of its future position will be in error.

2. One or more cycles which were stable have now become unstable, so that they are no longer included in the cycle sum.

3. One or more cycles which were unstable have now become stable.

In a program such as Channalyze, this can be checked by studying the distribution of cycles each day as new data arrives. If the distribution remains the same, then that is a positive outcome. However, it is still necessary to check the amplitude and wavelength of each stable cycle to check for consistency.

Number of different cycles

Small number of cycles

The analysis of the stable cycles present in a stock price movement may show anything from just two major ones up to around 20 within the range of five days to 300 days. Figure 13.8 shows the distribution of cycles in the British American Tobacco stock price.

Figure 13.8 – The distribution of stable cycles in British American Tobacco. There are two main groups of cycles. One is centred around a wavelength of 100 days, while the other is centred around a wavelength of 25 days. Cycles within the 100-day group are essentially the same.

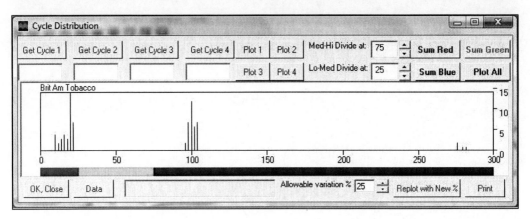

There are two main groups of cycles present. The group around a wavelength of 100 days is essentially the same cycle with a small change of a day or so in the estimation of wavelength from adjacent scans making it appear as multiple cycles. The same applies to the group at around 25 days. However, in this case, a change of one day in wavelength is of course a much larger percentage, so that each cycle in this group will bottom out or top out at different points.

As will be seen shortly, the best way forward in these situations is to sum the cycles in each of these groups to average out the variations.

In Figure 13.9 is shown the 20-day cycle. For much of its history it can be seen to have been unstable.

Figure 13.9 – The 20-day stable cycle in British American Tobacco. The vertical line shows the last calculated point of the cycle. The extrapolation to the right of this is a sine wave based on the recent wavelength and amplitude. The extrapolation is only valid for a few sweeps of the cycle and not for several months as shown here.

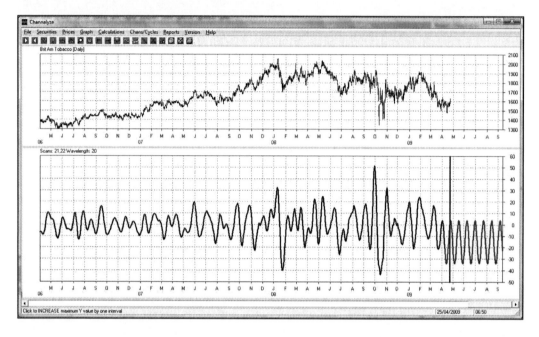

A better impression of its more recent stable phase can be obtained from the expanded chart shown in Figure 13.10. It can be seen now that the cycle has only been stable for two sweeps and that before that point it was very unstable. The message from this particular cycle is that its extrapolation is only going to be valid for a short period of time into the future.

Figure 13.10 – An expanded section of Figure 13.9 now shows the behaviour of the 20-day cycle in British American Tobacco more clearly. The left-hand vertical line shows the last calculated point of the cycle. The right-hand vertical line shows the position of the latest data point. The extrapolation goes from the left-hand vertical line and into the future.

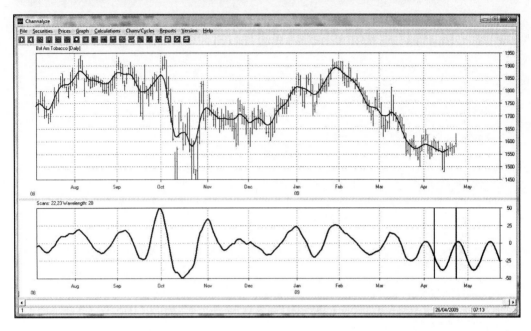

The 100-day cycle is a different matter, as can be seen in Figure 13.11. Here we have an excellent example of a cycle which has been stable for the whole of 2008. The extrapolation of the cycle from the last true calculated point (shown by the left-hand vertical line) now has a high degree of confidence in its future position. The extrapolation suggests that the cycle has already bottomed out on 1 April 2009 and is on the way up at the position of the latest point, which is 23 April 2009. It should top out on 9 June 2009.

Figure 13.11 – The behaviour of the 100-day cycle in British American Tobacco. The right-hand vertical line shows the position of the most recent data point. The left-hand vertical line shows the point from which the extrapolation of the cycle commences.

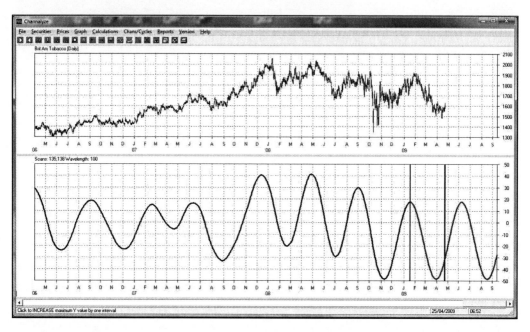

The sum of all stable cycles is shown in the lower panel of Figure 13.12. For ease of comparison the data has been left out of the plot in the upper panel, which now just shows the comparator of the nine-day centred average. The cycle sum is almost an exact replicate of the comparator up to the point where the comparator terminates four days in the past.

Figure 13.12 – The sum of all stable cycles in British American Tobacco. The nine-day centred average comparator is shown in the upper panel. The left-hand vertical line shows the point from which the highest wavelength cycle has been extrapolated. The middle vertical line shows the point from which the shortest wavelength cycle has been extrapolated. The right-hand vertical line is the position of the latest data point. A rise in the trend in the near future is forecast.

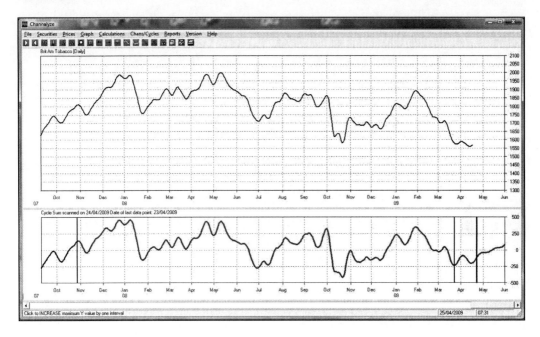

Remarkably, this replication is valid for some seventeen months. There must therefore be a very high probability that the estimation of the path that will be taken by the comparator, i.e. the nine-point average, in the near future will also be correct.

The trough on 14 April which has just been formed in the nine-day cycle is replicated in the cycle sum, which can be seen to have risen from this trough to the present time and is still forecast to continue to rise in the near future. Not shown in Figure 13.12 is the expected topping out of the cycle sum around 1 June 2009. This is in advance of the topping point for the 100-day cycle (9 June) because the short-term cycles are expected to top out prior to this date and the additive effect brings the maximum to this point.

It should be noted that since we have seen that the short-term cycles are only expected to be valid for a short time, this exact top determined from the cycle sum will be subject to a degree of uncertainty. However, the positive message from this cycle sum is that we can expect the trend to be rising until at least late May. Since this analysis was performed on 23 April, this means that the trader can expect around a month of rising trend. Naturally, as pointed out elsewhere in this book, the price itself will oscillate around this trend. Channel analysis will help to pin down buying and selling points over this future period.

It needs to be pointed out that just because there are only a few cycles present in the data, it does not follow that the extrapolation of the trend will be consistent with the comparator. Figure 13.13 shows the distribution of the cycles in Air Products. It can be seen that there are mainly two groups of cycles, with wavelengths around 26 days and 198 days. A few other cycles can be seen with wavelengths between 100 days and 150 days.

Figure 13.13 – The cycle distribution in Air Products at 23 April 2009.

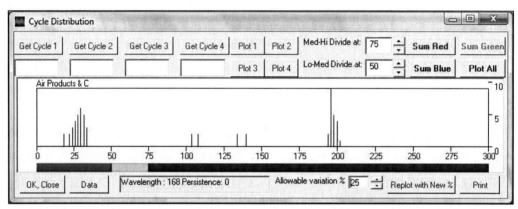

The cycle sum from this distribution is shown in Figure 13.14. It can be seen quite clearly that although there was an excellent correlation between the cycle sum and the comparator up to the position of the trough seen in mid-March, from this point onwards the cycle sum does not replicate the comparator up to 23 April. Thus the prediction beyond the last data point and the near future is not valid and must not be trusted.

Figure 13.14 – The sum of all stable cycles in Air Products as at 23 April 2009. The nine-day centred average comparator is shown in the upper panel. The left-hand vertical line shows the point from which the highest wavelength cycle has been extrapolated. The vertical line at the right is the position of the latest data point.

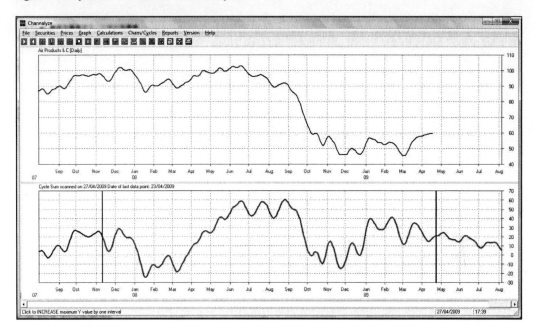

It would now be logical to assume that the cycle sum only replicates the comparator on those few occasions when there are only a few cycles present. Where there are a large number of cycles it would be logical to think that there is a greater chance of some of these becoming unstable in their extrapolated portion, so that any prediction will not be valid. The large number of cycles present in Agilent Technology is shown in Figure 13.15.

Figure 13.15 – The cycle distribution in Agilent Technology at 23 April 2009. There are a great many cycles present.

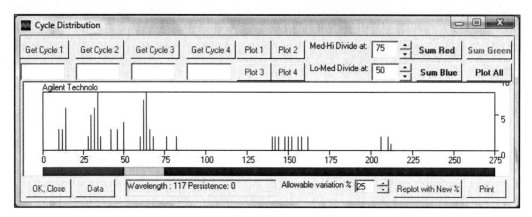

It is not surprising, therefore, that the cycle sum does not replicate the comparator from late in March until the last data point on April 23 (Figure 13.16). The cycle sum is seen to be falling while the comparator was rising until it terminated four days in the past. The explanation for the failure of the cycle sum to follow the comparator right up to the cut-off point in the comparator in both Air Products and Agilent Technology must be that an important stable cycle has now become unstable. Since the cycle sum will be more reactive to a change in the wavelength and hence the position of the next peak or trough, the assumption must be that a short-term cycle has now changed, in fact it might have disappeared altogether.

Figure 13.16 – The sum of all stable cycles in Agilent Technology as at 23 April 2009. The nine-day centred average comparator is shown in the upper panel. The left-hand vertical line shows the point from which the highest wavelength cycle has been extrapolated. The vertical line at the right is the position of the latest data point.

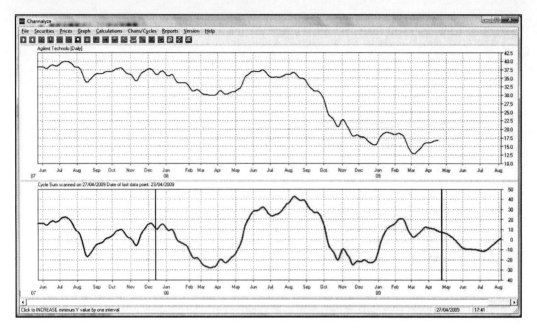

While it is logical to assume that a large number of stable cycles implies that the extrapolation is subject to a large error, this is not always the case. Thus in Hercules Inc. there is a large number of cycles of short wavelength, as well as some groups with wavelengths around 75 days and another of around 175 days, as can be seen in Figure 13.17.

Figure 13.17 – The cycle distribution in Hercules Inc. at 23 April 2009. There are a great many cycles present, especially those with short wavelengths.

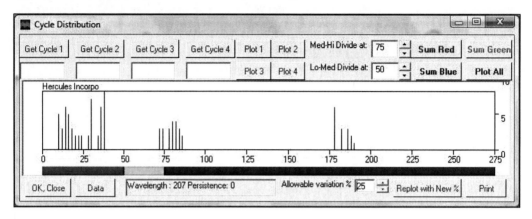

However, the cycle sum as shown in Figure 13.18 is a very good replicate of the comparator over the very long period from July 2007 to November 2008. While the prediction is for a small downturn within the next few days, followed by a rise, the influence of the large number of very short-term cycles extends much further into the near future than it is sensible to extrapolate. The reason for this lengthy extrapolation is because the cycles of wavelengths around 175 are normally extrapolated for about one wavelength into the future, taking us to June 2009. Because of the large number of short-term cycles, this extrapolation would only be taken to be valid for the next few weeks.

Figure 13.18 – The sum of all stable cycles in Hercules Inc. as at 23 April 2009. The nine-day centred average comparator is shown in the upper panel. The left-hand vertical line shows the point from which the highest wavelength cycle has been extrapolated. The vertical line at the right is the position of the latest data point. See text for comment on the future extrapolation.

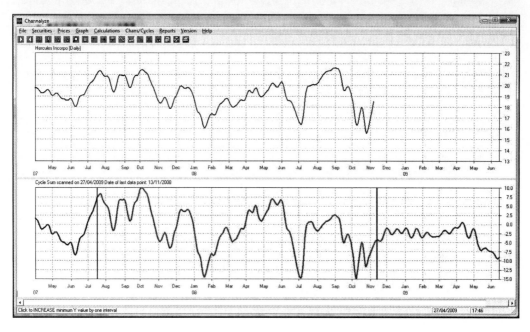

The ideal situation for summing stable cycles is when we have a small number of tight groups of cycles. This position is exemplified by the distribution shown for Ball Corporation in Figure 13.19.

Figure 13.19 – The cycle distribution in Ball Corporation at 23 April 2009. There are three distinct cycles present. This is an ideal distribution.

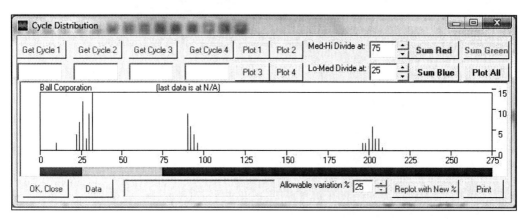

The expectation here is that the cycle sum will be extremely reliable. The plot of the cycle sum is shown in Figure 13.20. Our expectation is seen to be correct, since the cycle sum is almost a perfect replicate of the comparator. Note also the small range of oscillation of the price data around the comparator. This means that a good prediction of the future trend will give an excellent prediction of the range within which the price will be contained when the probability methods are employed.

Figure 13.20 – The sum of all stable cycles in Ball Corporation as at 23 April 2009. The nine-day centred average comparator is shown in the upper panel. The vertical line at the right is the position of the latest data point. All of the cycle sum trace to the left of this line is the result of extrapolation.

It is helpful in these examples to show how valid the extrapolation of the cycle sum, and hence the trend, was at the time by calculating the comparator far enough in the future that we have the true values for the trend as given by the nine-day average. This situation is followed for Wolseley in Figures 13.21 to 13.24.

It can be seen in Figure 13.21 that while the important group of cycles is grouped around a wavelength of 70-80 days, there are also high wavelengths present within the range 150 to 300 days. At this point in time (November 2008) the cycle sum agrees very well with the comparator, as shown in Figure 13.22.

Figure 13.21 – The cycle distribution in Wolseley at 28 November 2008.

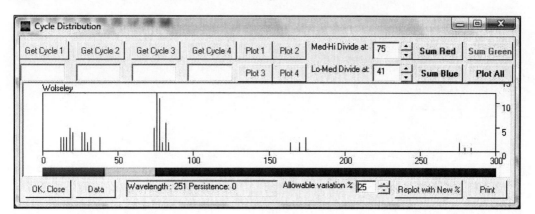

Figure 13.22 – The cycle sum for Wolseley calculated on 28 November 2008. The comparator is shown in the upper panel. The vertical line at the right in the lower panel is the position of the latest data point. The section of the cycle sum shown above is extrapolated.

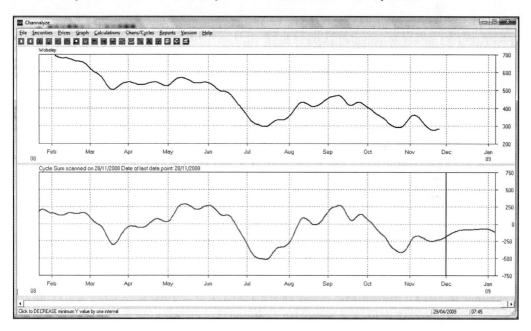

Viewed at from a much later point in time (23 April 2009), where we now have the benefit of the true calculation of the comparator, it can be seen that the extrapolated cycle sum in the lower panel of Figure 13.23, taken from Figure 13.22, is almost identical with the true comparator shown in the upper panel of Figure 13.23.

This is an excellent example that confirms the usefulness of this method of trend prediction.

Figure 13.23 – The upper panel shows the true value of the nine-day average calculated at 23 April 2009. The lower panel shows the cycle sum calculated in November 2008. The two plots are of almost identical shape. Note that the vertical scales are of necessity different.

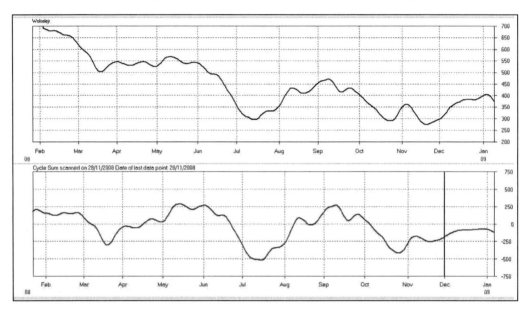

It is interesting to see the cycle distribution calculated on 23 April 2009. This is shown in Figure 13.24. The wavelength axes are now different for the reason that the high wavelengths remarked on earlier are now absent. However, the group of cycles of wavelength between 70 and 80 days remains essentially the same while there are some new cycles of wavelengths between 50 and 60 days.

Figure 13.24 – The cycle distribution in Wolseley at 23 April 2009.

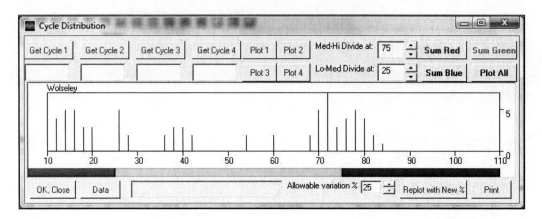

This change in the distribution would be expected to affect the cycle sums, making them differ from the true value. However, the change in the stable cycles shown in Figure 13.24 did not happen until March 2009, so that the original cycle distribution remained in effect for around four months. Thus the prediction in November remained valid.

The cycle distribution in United Utilities is shown in Figure 13.25. Again, we have the favourable position that there are only a few groups of cycles and the main groups are quite widely separated in wavelength. We would therefore expect that the cycle sum would replicate the comparator quite closely. This is indeed the case as shown by the plots in Figure 13.26.

Figure 13.25 – The cycle distribution in United Utilities at 28 November 2009.

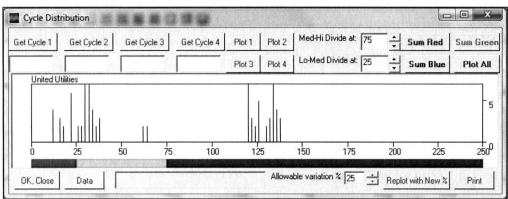

What is interesting about this chart (13.25) is that the prediction is for the cycle sum to bottom out and then rise for a short period, fall back and then rise again.

Figure 13.26 – The cycle sum in United Utilities on 28 November 2008.

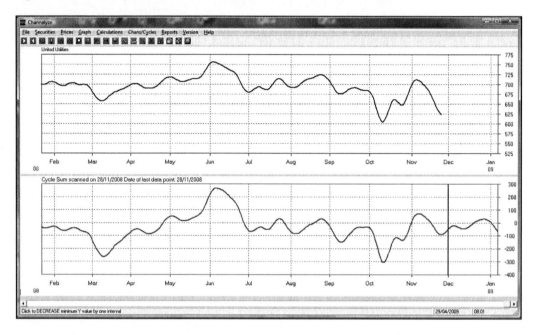

By 23 April 2009, the actual progress of the comparator enables a comparison to be made with the predicted cycle sum shown in Figure 13.27.

Figure 13.27 – The cycle sum in United Utilities on 23 April 2009. The comparator can now be compared with the predicted cycle sum in Figure 13.26.

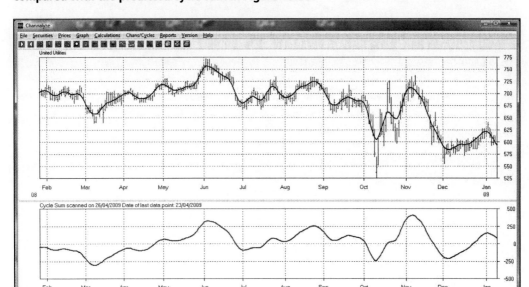

The predicted turning points in the cycle sum are compared with the actual turning points in the comparator nine-day centred average and are shown in Table 13.1. Bearing in mind that the prediction was carried out in November the agreement is astonishing, with some predictions being exactly right and those that are incorrect are only a few days out, even as far into the future as the end of January.

Table 13.1 – Predicted turning points in the cycle sum compared with actual turning points in the nine-day centred average.

Trough/peak	Predicted date	Actual date
Trough	12 October 2008	10 October 2008
Peak	20 October 2008	20 October 2008
Peak	7 November 2008	6 November 2008
Peak	29 December 2009	2 January 2009
Trough	12 January 2009	16 January 2009
Peak	21 January 2009	21 January 2009
Peak	5 February 2009	10 February 2009

Cycles are present in all markets and the value of cycle sums in predicting future trends is equally valid whatever the market, with the proviso that in most markets only around 10% of the securities are passing through a phase where their cycles are predictable. Thus in the Australian market we show the position in Figure 13.28 of CSL Ltd, a bio-pharmaceutical company, at three different points in time in 2009.

Figure 13.28 – The cycle sum for CSL Ltd calculated on 9 January 2009. The vertical line at the right is the position of the latest data point. The section of the cycle sum between the two vertical lines is extrapolated.

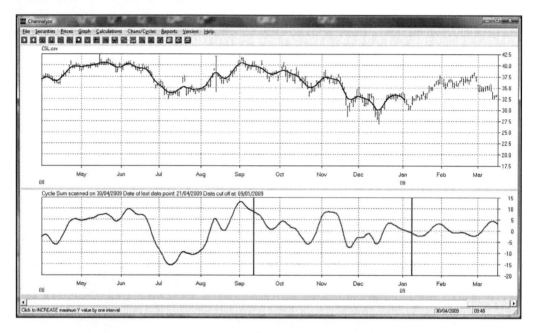

We can see from the subsequent movement of the price data after 9 January that the predicted trend is compatible with the price movement. The comparator is also in agreement with the cycle sum. Thus the cycles in CSL are remaining stable. This is also the case for the position in February 2009 (Figure 13.29) and April 2009 (Figure 13.30).

Figure 13.29 – The cycle sum for CSL Ltd calculated on 4 February 2009. The vertical line at the right is the position of the latest data point. The section of the cycle sum between the two vertical lines is extrapolated.

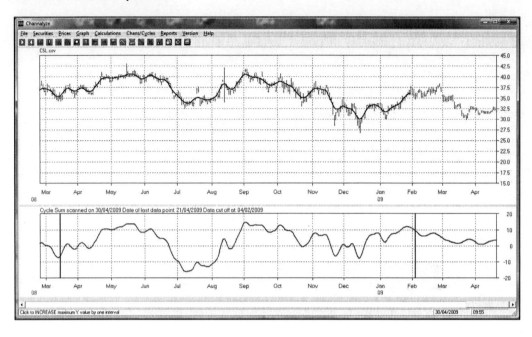

Figure 13.30 – The cycle sum for CSL Ltd calculated on 21 April 2009. The vertical line at the right is the position of the latest data point. The section of the cycle sum between the two vertical lines is extrapolated.

Failure of Extrapolations

It is interesting to study the changes which occur in the number and wavelengths of the stable cycles between two points in time which are reasonably far apart. In the case of Rolls-Royce, the position on the 23 April shown in Figure 13.31 can be compared with the position six months earlier on 2 February 2009 in Figure 13.32.

Figure 13.31 – The distribution of stable cycles in Rolls-Royce on 23 April 2009.

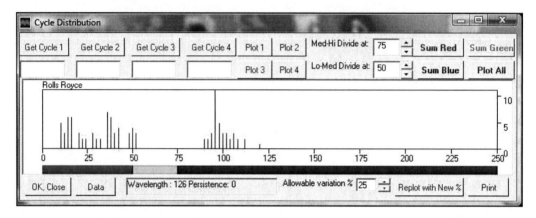

Figure 13.32 – The distribution of stable cycles in Rolls-Royce on 2 February 2009.

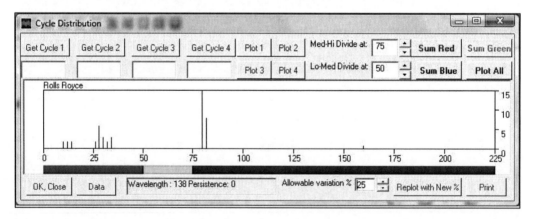

It can be seen that there is such an enormous difference between the two cycle sums that they would appear not to be from the same security. The peaks grouped around a wavelength of 96 days in April were totally absent in February, as were the peaks of wavelengths less than 25 days. On the other hand, the peaks of wavelengths 80 and 82 present in February are not present in April. It is not surprising therefore that with such a drastic difference in the number and wavelength of stable cycles between the two points in time that the two extrapolations of the cycle sums are also quite different. These two are compared in Figure 13.33.

Figure 13.33 – The cycle sum on 2 February 2009 (upper panel) compared with the cycle sum on 23 April (lower panel).

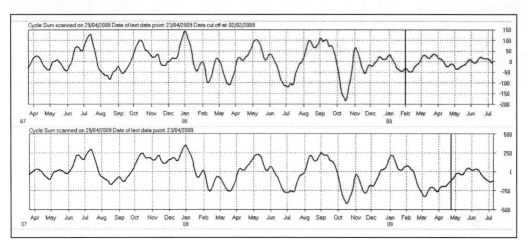

The predictions couldn't be more different. In February the prediction is for a small fall followed by a rise, whereas in April the prediction for the same section of time is for a large fall. It will of course be several months into the future before the true value for the comparator can be obtained.

When the cycle sum obtained in February is judged against the comparator (Figure 13.34), it is seen to be consistent. The peak on 5 January in the sum occurs two days before the peak in the comparator, but this is only a minor difference. Thus there is no reason to believe at this point that the prediction for a rise in the trend in the near future is other than correct.

Quite clearly, since the subsequent movement of the price is in the opposite direction, we would have made a major mistake in basing a trading decision on the position on 2 January.

Figure 13.34 – The cycle sum for Rolls-Royce on 2 February 2009 (lower panel) is consistent with the comparator (upper panel).

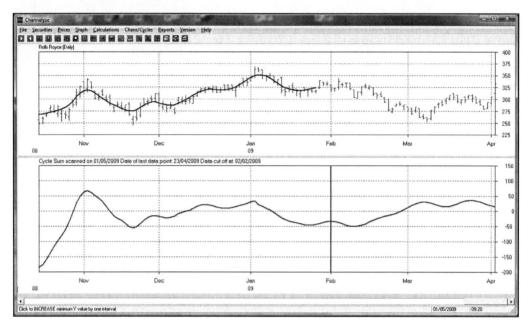

It is always necessary to recalculate the cycle sum each day as the new daily close value becomes available. This will usually show immediately when the cycle sum no longer agrees with the comparator. However, in the case of Rolls-Royce this did not happen. For the next ten days or so, the extrapolation of the cycle sum gave the same prediction of a minor peak followed by a longer rise.

The question therefore arises as to how we can avoid such situations in which the cycle sum is giving the wrong prediction. The problem is that there is nothing in the properties of the stable cycles themselves which will give an indication of the wrong prediction. The answer lies in confirmation of the prediction by using probability and channel analysis, as discussed in the next chapter.

14

Bringing it All Together

Although the primary predictive tool is the cycle sum, we saw in the last chapter that it is dangerous to rely on just this when taking a trading decision. There is a logical sequence that must be followed if consistent success is to be obtained.

Four Key Steps

If you have a software package that will calculate cycle sums and channels, the steps are:

1. Get the cycle sum, as discussed in Chapter 13, and make sure that the cycle sum is as close as possible in shape to the comparator nine-day centred average. As we mentioned previously, only about 10% of the securities in any one market will satisfy this test.

2. If the cycle sum agrees with the comparator, construct the 51-day and 101-day channels. Analyse these using the principles discussed in Chapters 11 and 12. We are looking for a value of the security having just retreated from a boundary. Retreat from the lower boundary signifies a probable rise; retreat from the upper boundary signifies a probable fall.

3. If the channel analysis confirms the outcome expected from the cycle sum, use the probability analysis method discussed in Chapter 4 for the estimated price range five days into the future.

4. If the estimated position of the trend of interest five days into the future lies within the probable price range and somewhere near the middle, then all probabilities are favourable to take a position.

If you do not have a software package that will calculate cycle sums and channels, the steps are:

1. Use the methods described to obtain three key cycles. Good general values are 25-day (use the difference between 21- and 29-day triangularly weighted centred averages), 75-day (use the difference between 65- and 85-day triangularly weighted centred averages) and 151-day cycles (use the difference between 131- and 171-day triangularly weighted centred averages). Many packages will allow you to create your own indicators so that you can take the difference between two centred averages. Make sure that you take the correct difference – it is the value of the shorter-term average minus the value for the longer-term average at each point in time. Also plot the nine-day centred average as the comparator.

2. Use your software package to plot the 51-day and 101-day centred averages. Using a piece of paper and a pencil on a printout of this chart, draw lines an equal distance above and below each average so as to end up with channels which contain the vast majority of the day-to-day movement of the security. Your paper-and-pencil channels can be analysed in exactly the same way as discussed in Chapters 11 and 12.

3. If you have the time and patience, you can construct the five-day distributions of the price changes and estimate the probable price range five days into the future.

You will now have replicated, as closely as possible, the procedure followed by readers who have a package which calculates cycle sums and channels.

Although we have frequently mentioned that only about 10% of securities will pass the first test of having stable, predictable cycles, this should be a large enough pool to end up with several securities that have passed all of the tests for a high probability near-future movement.

The rest of this chapter will look at various examples. In some of these, only the first one or two tests will be passed, whereas others will pass all of the tests.

Securities failing test #1

Using cycle sums – 3i Group (London)

Figure 14.1 shows the position in 3i Group (London Market) on 11 May 2009. Quite clearly there is no correlation between the cycle sum and the comparator over the last few weeks. There is a trough in the comparator on 30 April which is not replicated in the cycle sum. This stock therefore fails at the first test and no further analysis would be carried out at this point in time.

Figure 14.1 – The cycle sum in 3i Group as determined on 11 May 2009. There is no correlation between the recent cycle sum and the nine-day centred average used as the comparator. This security would not be taken forward as a possible trading situation.

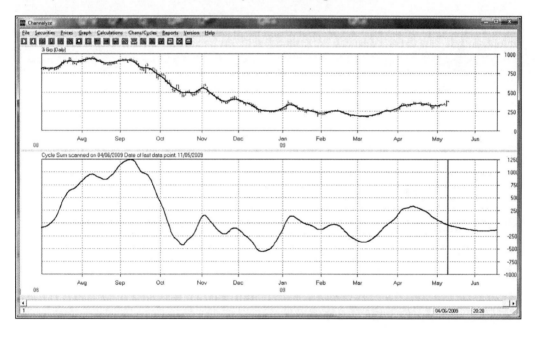

In the absence of cycle scanning software, a plot of the three key cycles will also help to decide if the security fails the first test. As mentioned earlier, those software packages which allow the user to define their own indicators will provide these data.

A plot of these for 3i Group is shown in Figure 14.2. The point of interest is the fact that the comparator turned up at the very end of April.

Figure 14.2 – The 25-day, 75-day and 151-day cycles in 3i Group as determined on 11 May 2009. Visually it can be seen that the sum of these three cycles over the previous month should continue to fall, and the upward turn in the comparator at the very end of April would not be replicated in the sum of the three key cycles. This security would not be taken forward as a possible trading situation.

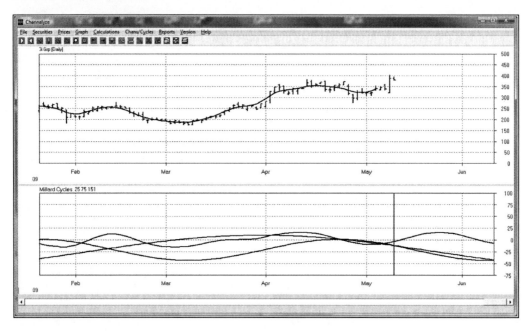

Using key cycles – 3i Group

A visual estimate of the sum of the three key cycles shown in the lower panel of Figure 14.2 would produce a falling trend, not replicating the behaviour of the comparator. This method therefore also removes this stock from further consideration.

Using cycle sums – Analog Devices (New York)

A plot of Analog Devices from the New York market is shown in Figure 14.3. Between April and May the cycle sum can be seen to be gently falling, while the comparator is gently rising.

Figure 14.3 – The cycle sum in Analog Devices as determined on 11 May 2009. There is no correlation between the recent cycle sum and the nine-day centred average used as the comparator.

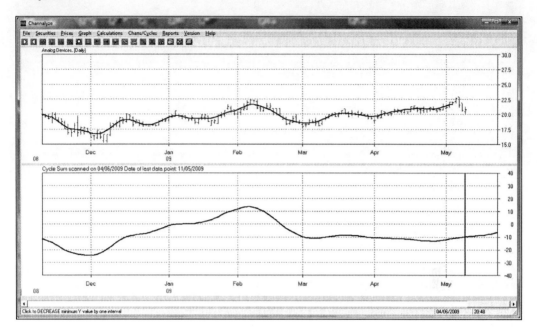

There is also the point that over the last four days the data itself is falling. This would be expected to have caused a minor blip in the cycle sum at this point, and this is not present. This stock therefore also fails at the first test and no further analysis would be carried out at this point in time.

When the distribution of cycles is examined, it can be seen (Figure 14.4) that there are a great many cycles present from a wavelength of seven days up to a wavelength of 104 days. As was mentioned in Chapter 13, this type of cycle distribution is to be avoided.

Figure 14.4 – The stable cycle distribution in Analog Devices as determined on 11 May 2009. Securities with so many stable cycles should be avoided.

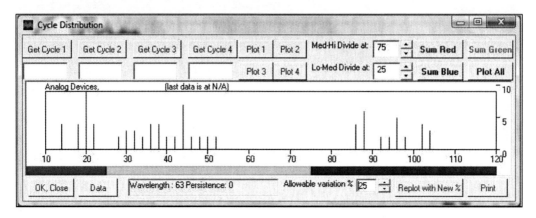

Using key cycles – Analog Devices

When the three key cycles are plotted as shown in Figure 14.5, we might reach a different conclusion.

Figure 14.5 – The recent section of the 25-day, 75-day and 151-day cycles in Analog Devices is shown in the lower panel as determined on 11 May 2009. A visual estimation of the recent sum of these three cycles would give a similar profile to that of the comparator.

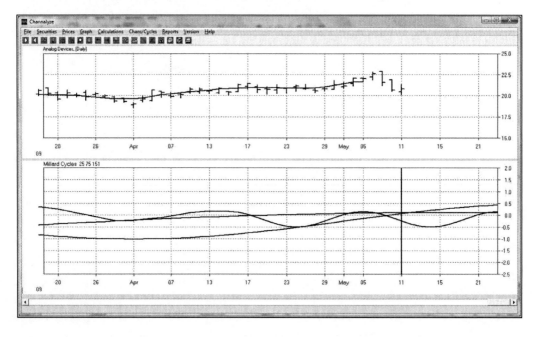

A simple visual estimate of the sum of the three key cycles which are shown in the lower panel would lead to the view that this sum is gently rising, in accordance with the comparator. We also see that the fall in the stock price over the last four days is confirmed by the fall in the more responsive 25-day cycle in the lower panel.

Traders using this approach would therefore need to perform the second test using channels.

The 51-day channel is shown in Figure 14.6, along with the 75-day cycle. It can be seen that while the trough in the cycle and the trough in the channel are not quite aligned in time, the implication is that the channel is rising as shown. The alignment will not be exact, of course, because while the 75-day cycle plot is showing only that cycle, the channel is showing the sum of all cycles with wavelengths greater than 51 days.

Figure 14.6 – The 51-day channel is now shown for Analog Devices on 11 May 2009. The lower panel shows just the 75-day cycle. The relationship between the price level and the lower boundary is now at a critical point.

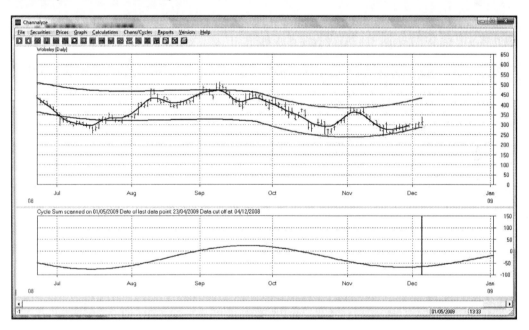

More important is the fact that the price has approached the lower boundary of the channel. It will be a few more days before it will become clear whether the price will penetrate the lower boundary. If it does, then the boundary will have to be adjusted downwards. If this is the case then no decision should be taken – never initiate a trade when a boundary has had to be adjusted. If the price does not penetrate the lower boundary and instead bounces upwards, then there is the potential to open a trade.

Securities failing test #2

Using cycle sums – Associated British Foods (London)

Figure 14.7 shows the cycle sum for Associated British Foods, determined from data which terminated on 11 May 2009. It can be seen quite clearly that the cycle sum is a good replicate of the nine-day centred average used as the comparator. This security therefore passes test #1, and attention will now pass to test #2, using channel analysis.

Figure 14.7 – The cycle sum in Associated British Foods as determined on 11 May 2009. The cycle sum over the recent past replicates the comparator.

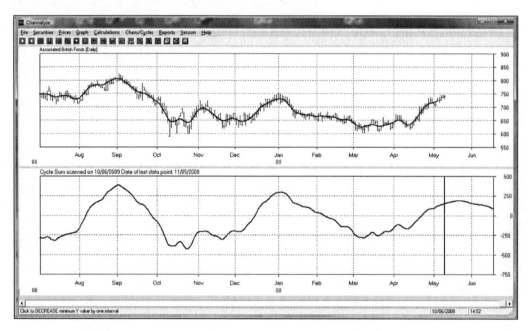

Using key cycles – Associated British Foods

Figure 14.8 shows the three key cycles of wavelength 25, 75 and 151 days. Quite clearly a visual summation of these three will be in broad agreement with the comparator, so that the security passes test #1. Again attention will pass to test #2, using channel analysis.

Figure 14.8 – The recent section of the 25-day, 75-day and 151-day cycles in Associated British Foods is shown in the lower panel as determined on 11 May 2009. A visual summation would agree with the comparator.

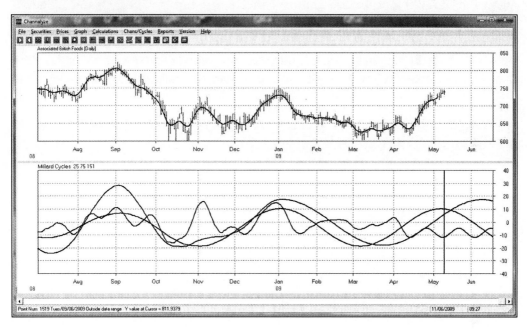

Channel analysis – Associated British Foods

The 51-day channel is shown in Figure 14.9. The extrapolation of the channel to the latest date gives no indication that it is about to top out, whereas the cycle sum shown in Figure 14.7 does indicate that we are near the top of the trend. Although the channel could be adjusted by the methods discussed in Chapter 12, the current set of data would lead to a range of possible adjustments. One extreme would be to increase the upward bend even more to bring the latest price value to the lower boundary, while the other extreme would be to decrease the bend in the channel to cause the recent high value at the end of April to approach the upper boundary. In such an ambiguous situation, no decision would be taken.

Figure 14.9 – The 51-day channel is now shown for Associated British Foods on 11 May 2009. There is no indication that the channel is about to top out, as predicted by the cycle sum shown in Figure 14.7.

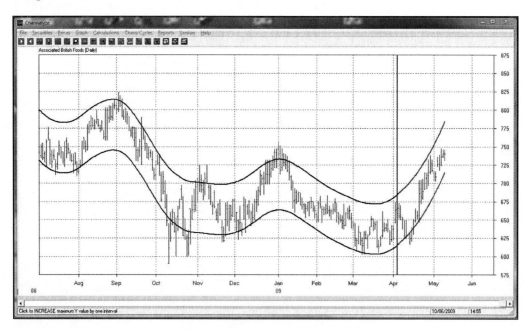

Using cycle sums – Cape Lambert Iron Ore (Sydney)

The cycle sum for this security as determined on 4 June 2009 is shown in Figure 14.10. As can be seen, the cycle sum is a good replicate of the comparator over the whole time period covered by the plot. The extrapolated trend is headed downwards.

Since this security has passed test #1, it is now necessary to carry out test #2, which is an analysis of the channel. We expect the channel to follow the direction of the extrapolated cycle sum.

Using key cycles – Cape Lambert Iron Ore (Sydney)

The three key cycles for this security are shown in Figure 14.11. It can be seen that a visual summation would give a reasonably close agreement with the comparator which is shown in the upper panel.

Figure 14.10 – The cycle sum in Cape Lambert Iron Ore as determined on 4 June 2009. The cycle sum over the recent past replicates the comparator.

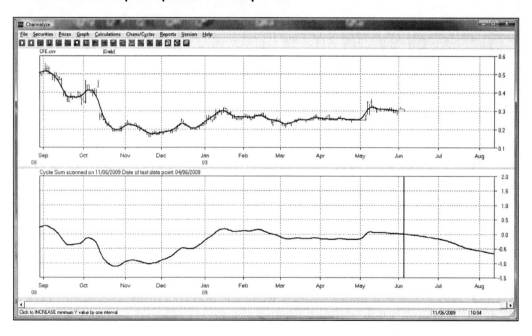

The small peak in the 25-day cycle around the middle of May is also seen in the comparator, and the fall in the comparator after that peak is obviously echoed by the fall in both the 75-day and 151-day cycles. Therefore this security passes test #1 and has to be checked against test #2.

Channel analysis – Cape Lambert Iron Ore

The 51-day channel of this security is shown in Figure 14.12. It can be seen that the extrapolated section of the channel from the vertical line is rising and is expected to do so over the immediate future.

Figure 14.11 – The 25-day, 75-day and 151-day cycles in Cape Lambert Iron Ore on 4 June 2009. A visual summation would be in reasonable agreement with the comparator.

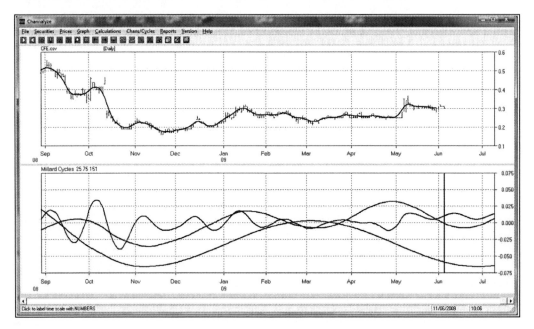

Figure 14.12 – The 51-day channel is now shown for Cape Lambert Iron Ore on 4 June 2009. There is no indication that the channel is about to top out, as predicted by the cycle sum shown in Figure 14.10.

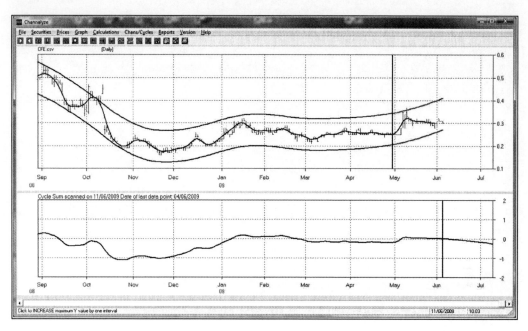

There is nothing in the placement of the data within the channel that gives any indication that the channel will begin to bend downwards. In fact, an interpretation of the expected price movement within the channel would be for a bounce upwards from the lower boundary.

Thus there is a complete disagreement between the message being given by the channel (whether it has been drawn by the program or drawn by hand) and that being given by the cycle sum.

Cape Lambert Iron Ore would therefore be abandoned at this point in time and attention would turn elsewhere.

Using cycle sums – Atagas Income Trust (Toronto)

The plot of the cycle sum in this security on 4 May 2009 is shown in Figure 14.13.

Figure 14.13 – The cycle sum in Atagas Income Trust as determined on 4 May 2009. The cycle sum over the recent past replicates the comparator.

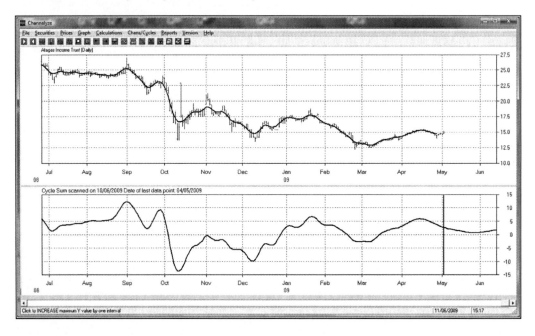

Once again, it can be seen that the cycle sum replicates the behaviour of the nine-day centred average used as the comparator. The peak in the middle of April in the comparator was replicated faithfully in the cycle sum, so that quite clearly this security passes test #1.

Using key cycles – Atagas Income Trust

The plot of these is shown in Figure 14.14. It should be noted that in this case the 151-day cycle terminates back in time. This is because in the period off to the left of the chart this cycle was irregular and could not be extrapolated up to the latest point in time. In spite of this, it can be seen that both the 25-day and 75-day cycles have been falling since mid-April and are expected to continue to fall over the next week or so.

Figure 14.14 – The recent section of the 25-day, 75-day and 151-day cycles in Atagas Income Trust is shown in the lower panel as determined on 4 May 2009. A visual summation would be in reasonable agreement with the comparator.

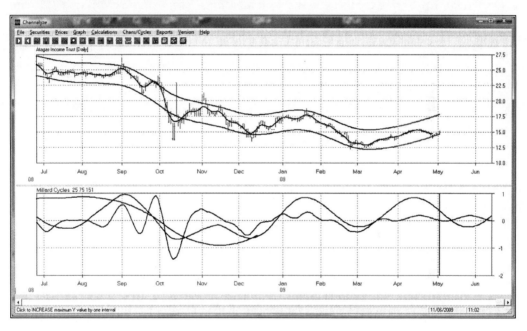

Channel analysis for Atagas Income Trust

The 51-day channel for Atagas Income Trust is shown in Figure 14.15. Quite clearly, the extrapolation of this channel from the cut-off point shown by the vertical line shows it to be rising. This extrapolation is a smooth continuation of the previous rate of bend of the channel. This upward direction for the channel is the opposite behaviour to that of the cycle sum which, as shown in Figure 14.13, was falling and predicted to continue to fall.

Because of this difference between the two tests, this security would be abandoned at this stage and another one sought which will pass the two tests.

Figure 14.15 – The 51-day channel is now shown for Atagas Income Trust on 4 May 2009. There is no indication that the channel should have topped out in mid-April, as predicted by the cycle sum shown in Figure 14.13.

Securities passing tests #1 and #2

Using cycle sums – Dover Corporation (New York)

A chart of Dover Corporation is shown in Figure 14.16. The data were acquired on 11 May 2009. The cycle sum in the lower panel is a good replicate of the comparator shown in the upper panel. The trough in early March in the comparator appears in the cycle sum at the same point in time, as does the peak in mid-April.

Figure 14.16 – The cycle sum in Dover Corporation as determined on 11 May 2009. The cycle sum over the recent past replicates the comparator.

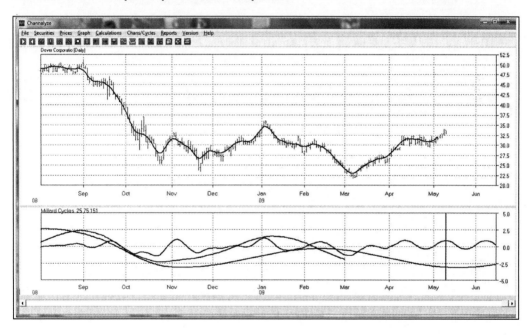

Since that point it can be seen that the cycle sum and the comparator are now rising. The cycle sum is estimated as continuing to rise for the next month or so. This security looks a good prospect for a rise from its present level, although the rise is not expected to be a rapid one, but rather a gentle upward progress.

Using key cycles – Dover Corporation

The three key cycles are shown in Figure 14.17. The 75-day cycle has not been extrapolated because it has an irregular appearance in the time span prior to that shown and the wavelength has varied more than the allowable amount. Even so, the 25-day cycle follows the path of the comparator over the last month, and the 151-day cycle appears to be bottoming out. Because of this the security would be taken to an analysis of the channel.

Figure 14.17 – The 25-day, 75-day and 151-day cycles in Dover Corporation on 11 May 2009. A visual summation would be in reasonable agreement with the comparator.

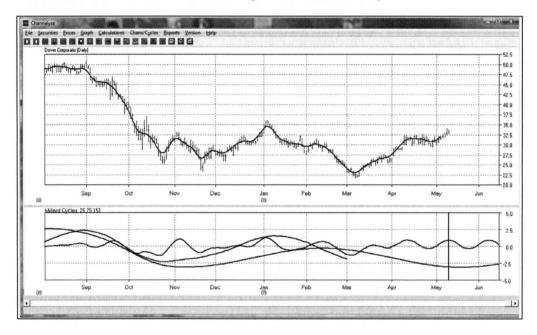

Channel analysis – Dover Corporation

As can be seen from Figure 14.18, the price is about to bounce up from the lower boundary, and the channel itself is rising. This means that the effect of the short-term trend and that of the longer-term trend are added, thereby increasing the potential gain.

Figure 14.18 – The 51-day channel is now shown for Dover Corporation on 11 May 2009. The indication is that the price is about to bounce upwards from the lower boundary of the channel which is itself rising, increasing the potential gain to be made.

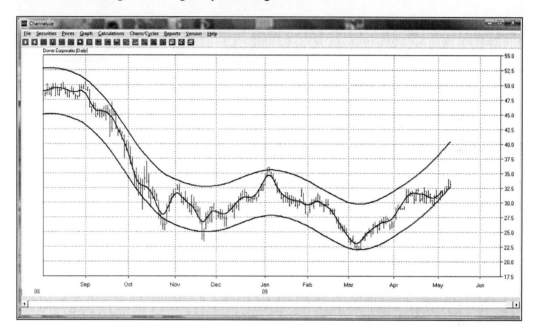

This security has therefore passed both of the tests for initiating a trade.

The final issue which can be addressed is the question of the probable price range five days ahead. Using the Millard version of the Monte Carlo simulation gives a range of $29.39 to $37.39 at the 90% level as discussed in Chapter 5. This range is shown in Figure 14.19.

Figure 14.19 – The vertical line shows the 90% probable price range for Dover Corporation predicted for five days ahead from 11 May 2009.

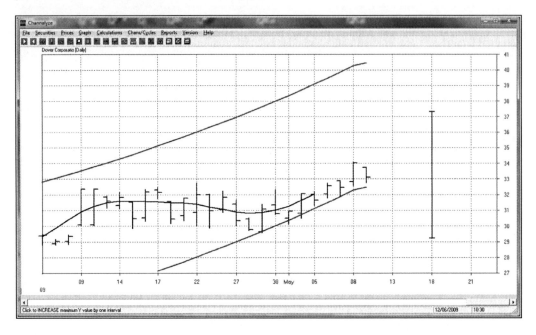

It can be seen that if the channel continues upwards on its predicted path, the 90% price range will make it very unlikely that the price will reach the top of the channel within this five-day period. There is also the probability that the price may fall below its current level. If that happens then of course the channel boundaries will have to be adjusted downwards to accommodate any price fall. As always, once a trade has been opened, the price movement must be followed very carefully on a daily basis.

Using cycle sums – Addax Petroleum (Toronto)

In Figure 14.20 is shown the cycle sum for Addax Petroleum on 4 May 2009. There is a good correspondence between the cycle sum and the comparator and it can be seen that the cycle sum is predicted to continue to rise over the next few weeks before topping out again. The peak in the comparator in mid-April is also replicated in the cycle sum, giving confidence in its validity.

Figure 14.20 – The cycle sum in Addax Petroleum as determined on 4 May 2009. The cycle sum over the recent past replicates the comparator.

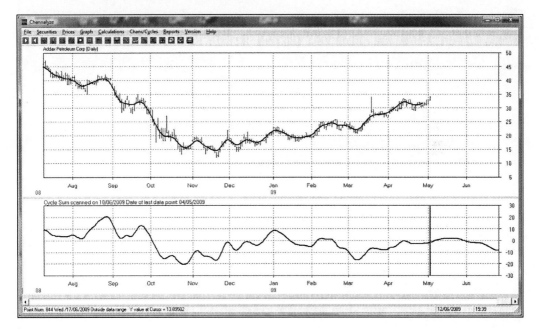

Using key cycles – Addax Petroleum

Two of the key cycles, the 25-day and 75-day, are shown in Figure 14.21. In this case there was not enough data present to be able to isolate and extrapolate the 151-day cycle. The message from these two cycles is that the short-term 25-day cycle is about to turn up, while the longer term 75-day cycle is expected to top out very soon. The additive effect of these two is that a short-term rise is in the offing, but that its rise will be limited by the fact that the long-term trend is about to end. Thus there is a potential for profit and the position of the channels in this security can be examined.

Figure 14.21 – The 25-day and 75-day cycles in Addax Petroleum on 4 May 2009. A visual summation of these would be in reasonable agreement with the comparator.

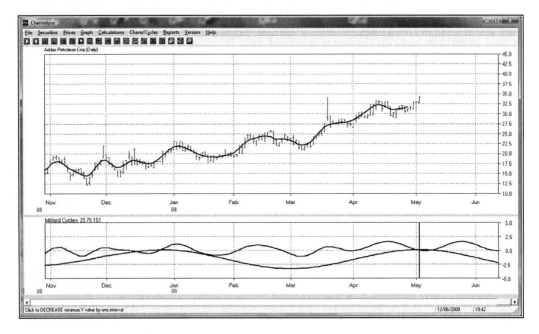

Channel analysis – Addax Petroleum

In Figure 14.22 is shown the 51-day channel for Addax Petroleum, determined on 4 May 2009. The price has just bounced up from the lower boundary, and if the position of the upper boundary is correct, the potential is for a rise to around CAN$38 over the next week or so. However, as we saw from the cycle sum, the longer-term trend will top out very soon. Because of this, the channel, which also reflects the long-term trend, is unlikely to continue for long in the direction indicated by the extrapolation. It should be remembered that all initial extrapolations of channels are simply the continuation of the curvature of the last few points of the actual channel. They do not take into account any change in direction which might become apparent when a closer inspection of the short-term features within the channel is carried out (as we saw in Chapters 11 and 12).

Figure 14.22 – The 51-day channel for Addax Petroleum on 4 May 2009. The indication is that the price is about to bounce upwards from the lower boundary of the channel.

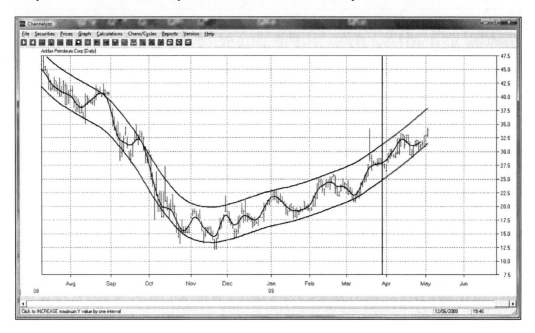

Another point to make is that the extrapolated channel is curving upwards at a slightly increasing rate. As such, therefore, it will never reach a maximum. Since all trends eventually change direction, while the immediate path of this channel makes sense, it cannot reflect the true picture for more than a week or two into the future.

In order to clarify this difficulty, a longer-term channel is needed, such as the 101-day channel shown in Figure 14.23. The message from this channel is more in line with the message from the cycle sum – that while there is a rise due in the short-term trend contained within the channel, this will take it to the upper boundary much sooner than was anticipated with the 51-day channel. Thus a position could be taken in Addax Petroleum with the proviso that the upper limit reached is probably CAN$36 to CAN$37.

Figure 14.23 – The 101-day channel is now shown for Addax Petroleum on 4 May 2009. The indication is that the price will shortly retreat from the upper boundary.

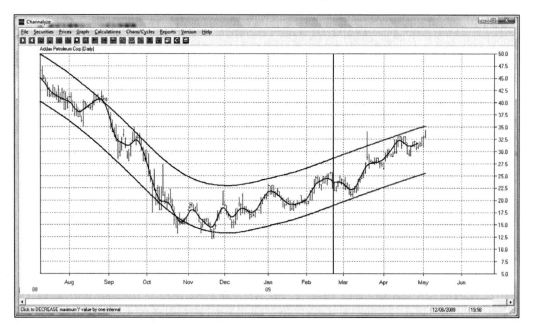

Finally, in Figures 14.24 and 14.25 we show the estimated price range five days ahead, along with the last few extrapolated boundaries of the two channels. As far as the relationship to the 51-day channel is concerned, we can see that there is no indication that the price five days hence will be at any particular point within the channel. In the case of the 101-day channel, we can see that it is very unlikely that the price will be near the lower boundary within five days. This use of the 90% probability range five days into the future is extremely valuable in adding more information to the behaviour of the short-term trends which are contained within the channel.

Figure 14.24 – The vertical line shows the 90% probable price range for Addax Petroleum predicted for five days ahead from 4 May 2009. Also shown is the 51-day channel.

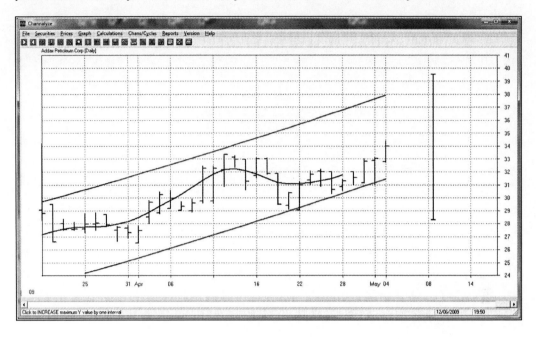

Figure 14.25 – The vertical line shows the 90% probable price range for Addax Petroleum predicted for five days ahead from 4 May 2009. Also shown is the 101-day channel.

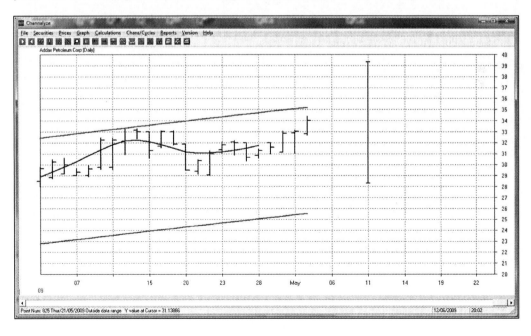

In some cases, as shown in Figure 14.25, it can put a restriction on the possible intra-channel movement which can occur in the immediate future. This is very helpful in deciding on the potential profit which might be made from a position and is a vindication of the necessity to study the three components of cycle sum, channels and probability range.

Using cycle sums – Coca-Cola Amatil Ltd (Sydney)

Figure 14.26 shows the cycle sum for Addax Petroleum on 9 June 2009. There is a good correspondence between the cycle sum and the comparator, and it can be seen that the cycle sum has already topped out and is predicted to continue to fall over the next few weeks. The peak in the comparator at the beginning of May is also replicated in the cycle sum. There is a difference in amplitude between the recent peak at the beginning of June in the cycle sum and the peak that appears to be in the process of formation in the comparator, but the general shape of these two plots is comparable.

Figure 14.26 – The cycle sum in Coca-Cola Amatil Ltd as determined on 9 June 2009. The cycle sum over the recent past replicates the comparator.

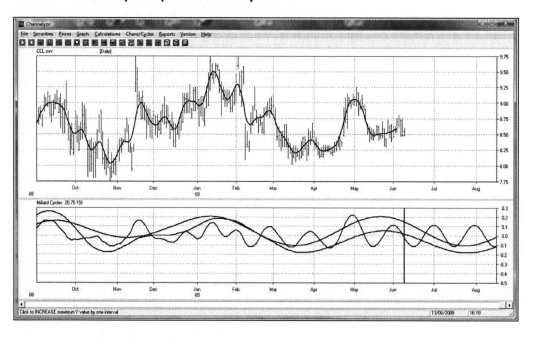

Using key cycles – Coca-Cola Amatil Ltd

The message from a plot of the three key cycles supports the conclusion obtained from the plot of the cycle sum. These cycles are shown in Figure 14.27. The 25-day cycle can be seen to be responsible for the peak in early May and the most recent one in early June. The fact that, overall, the long-term trends have topped out is confirmed by the behaviour of the 75-day and 151-day cycles, which both reached their maximum in the middle of May. Thus we expect an overall fall in the price of this security over the next few weeks.

Figure 14.27 – The 25-day, 75-day and 151-day cycles in Coca-Cola Amatil Ltd on 9 June 2009. A visual summation of these would be in reasonable agreement with the comparator. Overall, the longer-term trends illustrated by the 75-day and 151-day cycles have topped out.

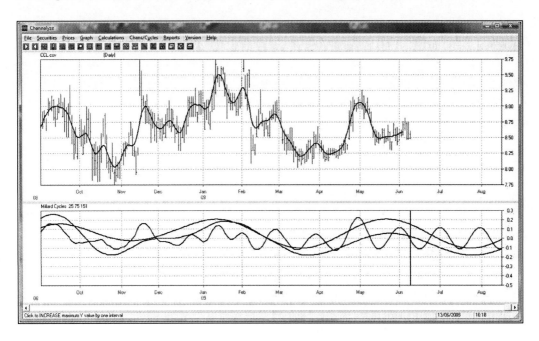

Channel analysis – Coca-Cola Amatil Ltd

The 51-day channel for this security is shown in Figure 14.28. Also shown in the lower panel are the key cycles, which were also shown in Figure 14.27. The vertical line in the upper panel, as always, denotes the start of the extrapolation of the channel.

Figure 14.28 – The 51-day channel for Coca-Cola Amatil Ltd on 9 June 2009. The indication is that the price is about to bounce downwards from the upper boundary of the channel.

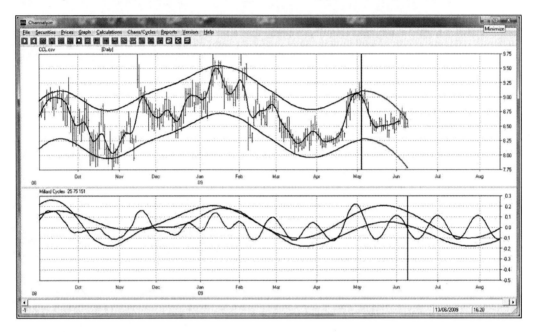

It can be seen that the extrapolation matches very closely the shape of the 75-day and 151-day cycles, giving added confidence that the channel position is valid. The only slight difference is that the peak in the channel formed by the extrapolation is slightly in front of the peaks in the cycles.

This coincidence of the channel and the long-term cycles at the time of writing is a strong indication of a fall in the price of this security from its current position over the next few weeks.

The plot of the 90% probable price range five days ahead as predicted by the Millard version of the Monte Carlo simulation is shown in Figure 14.29. A fall in price over the next five days would bring the price towards the lower end of this predicted price range. This is acceptable because the price of the security would still be contained within the extrapolated section of the channel.

Figure 14.29 – The vertical line shows the 90% probable price range for Coca-Cola Amatil Ltd predicted for five days ahead from 9 June 2009. Also shown is the 51-day channel.

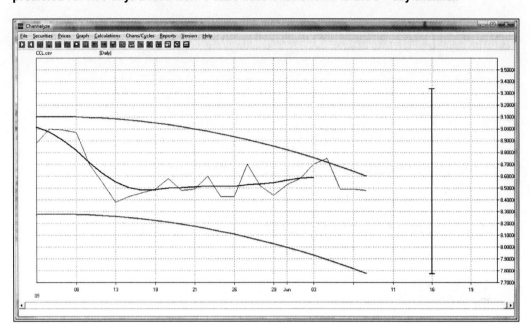

Conclusion

The examples in this chapter, taken from a variety of stock markets, will have shown the improvement obtained in the prediction of future price movement when all three components of the probability methods are employed together. While the general view of technical analysts is that virtually all securities can be analysed for future movement, the work in this book shows that this is not the case. Only a small number, around 10%, have cycles which extrapolation shows to be currently in a stable state and which therefore would appear to be predictable. However, the use of channel analysis will draw attention to those instances where the extrapolation is no longer valid, since one or more of the crucial cycles have become unstable over the period of extrapolation.

Finally, all extrapolations of cycles and channels are subject to error. It is the use of probability methods that will alert the trader to those situations in which probable movement is not in line with the movement predicted from cycle and channel analysis.

Index

B

Ball Corporation, as an example 225-226

Barclays, as an example 203

bin numbers 33, 116, 119-120

boundaries 119-121, 145

British American Tobacco, as an example 153-155, 203, 215-219

    short-term cycles in 156-170

Brunswick Corporation, as an example 145-149, 151-152

C

Cape Lambert Iron Ore, as an example 247-249

CCS Visions 2

centred averages 97-104, 114, 127

    boundaries and channels 119-124

    comparator 237

    compared with average differences 107

    data distribution around 114-115

    extrapolating 123-124

    numerical data 115-119

    probabilities from 114-124

channel

    analysis 2, 3, 6, 120, 122-124, 244, 246, 248, 252, 255, 259, 264

    bending of 146

    bottoming out 67, 137, 148-149

    boundaries 145, 155

    depth 146

    reducing 153-155

    direction, estimating 145-152

    dominant 205

    falling 187-202

    longer-term 205

    multiple 171

    rising 178

    shorter-term 170, 205

    short-term, very 172-174

    why does it work? 202-204

Channalyze 2, 7, 35-36, 121, 214

Channels & Cycles 1, 2

Coca-Cola Amatil Ltd 262-265

coin tossing 20-22

    sequence of 21-22

    standard deviation, formula for 21

Commonality Principle 72

cumulative distribution 34, 39

currency channels 165-170, 171, 172

CSL Ltd, as an example 232-233

cycles

    analysis 3

    definition of 3, 59

    extrapolation of 210-213

    key 240, 242-244, 245, 247, 251, 254, 258, 263

    market, and the 59-73, 66-71

      known cycles 71

    number of 214

    peaks and troughs, coincidence of 73

    stability 207, 218

    sums 210-215, 237, 239, 244, 247, 250, 253, 257, 262

cycloids 59-60

D

daily closes, markets 15-17

depth, constant 2, 6, 120, 145-146, 153

DJIA 15-17

distributions, converting to probabilities 32-34

Dover Corporation, as an example 253-256

drop points 92-93, 127, 130, 139

E

Eastman Kodak, as an example 137-138, 140-143

extrapolations

centred averages, and 123-124

failure of 234-236

moving averages 88

F

FTSE 100 15-17

future movement, simulating 45-57

H

Hercules Inc., as an example 223-225

H.J. Heinz Company, as an example 163-165

Hurst, J.M. 1, 72

I

intra-channel movements 175, 187

J

Jardine Lloyd Thompson, as an example 11, 22

L

lags 83, 97, 105

London daily closes 15-17

M

market

cycles, research on 71-73

risk 10-12

mean, the 29, 45

money management 9

Monte Carlo simulation 47-57

Millard version of 49-57, 131, 255-256, 264

Motorola, as an example 111- 113, 116, 118-119

moving averages 3, 83-87

applying to cycles 99-104

calculation of 91-104

data oscillation around 114

data smoothing, why 94-96

differences 104-107

extrapolating 88

lags, and 83